'An amazing, intricately detailed and personal history of the life of *hijras* and the modern-day trans community. From the glory of royal courts to the loss of respect and a fight for survival, this is a powerfully written exploration of sexuality, gender, Islam and South Asian culture.'

Madian Al Jazerah, author of *Are You This? Or Are You This?*

'A brave and compelling account of the author's transnational journey, interrogating questions of gender, faith, belonging and their complex intersections. It provides a fascinating lens through which to explore the politics of difference, gendered and otherwise, during these polarising times.'

Gayatri Reddy, Associate Professor of Anthropology and Gender & Women's Studies, University of Illinois Chicago

'Brimming with critical insight, this is a rich account of transfeminine experience, exploring political questions of faith, gender, race, sexuality and belonging, and highlighting how personal and social history enmesh. An important and timely intervention.'

Avtar Brah MBE, Professor Emerita of Sociology, Birkbeck, University of London

'A compelling narrative of transition, moving from rural Germany to South Asia, and located within a rich trajectory of trans folk in Islamic societies. Jagiella interweaves personal and political challenges, arguing for sexual and gender liberation across the world.'

Shahnaz Khan, Professor Emerita of Women and Gender Studies, Wilfred Laurier University, and author of *Transnational Feminism and the Moral Regulation of Pakistani Women*

AMONG THE EUNUCHS

LEYLA JAGIELLA

Among the Eunuchs

A Muslim Transgender Journey

HURST & COMPANY, LONDON

First published in the United Kingdom in 2021 by
C. Hurst & Co. (Publishers) Ltd.,
New Wing, Somerset House, Strand, London, WC2R 1LA
© Leyla Jagiella, 2021
All rights reserved.
Printed in the United Kingdom by Bell and Bain Ltd, Glasgow

Distributed in the United States, Canada and Latin America by
Oxford University Press, 198 Madison Avenue, New York, NY 10016,
United States of America.

A Cataloguing-in-Publication data record for this book
is available from the British Library.

ISBN: 9781787383876

This book is printed using paper from registered sustainable
and managed sources.

www.hurstpublishers.com

786

For my parents. We've been through a lot. But I am glad that we've made it.

And for all the young trans people who go through a lot right now. It will get better.

CONTENTS

ACKNOWLEDGEMENTS

This book would never have become a printable reality, had it not been for the tremendous help and support of many others. I won't be able to mention everybody by name here. But I want as many of you as possible to know how thankful I am for having you in my life and on this journey of writing. My greatest thanks have to go to my sisters in the hijra community in India, of course. The reader will have noticed that I rarely mention names and individual specifics in my book, for reasons that my sisters will understand best. But you are all remembered. My special prayers will always be for my sister Vandana, who sadly passed away several years ago. Equally great thanks go to my khwajasara and transgender sisters and friends in Pakistan. In particular to Neeli Rana, Zainy Chaudhary, Jiya Khan, Jannat Ali, Shehzadi Rai, Bebo Haider and Kami Sid who have all opened their doors and their hearts to me and have given me invaluable access to their world of experience. To Aisha Mughal and Mehlab Jameel for inspiring discussions both in the real world and online. Thanks also go to Sambhav Sharma and his wonderful mother who have shown me a different side of Delhi many years after my first stay in the city. It was the late filmmaker Khalid Gill who first brought me to Pakistan, and Danish-Pakistani filmmaker Saadat Munir who eventually brought me back, as part of the

ACKNOWLEDGEMENTS

Aks Film Festival. It was originally Anne Ogborn who introduced me to the community in India. Without these three my
journey through life may have looked quite different. More than
just thanks, but also a great load of respect I owe to the pioneers
of the global Queer Muslim world, whose work has informed my
own exploration of Islam and who have also so often given me
the space and occasion to make Muslim trans issues more visible.
Among them El-Farouk Khaki, Muhsin Hendricks, Dino
Suhonic and Scott Siraj al-Haqq Kugle. The Inclusive Mosque
Initiative in London—and there in particular Halima Gosai
Hussain, Asma Bhol and Naima Khan—have more than once
given me a platform to share my ideas and my knowledge and
their encouragement and friendship in particular has informed
this book more than they would probably know. The same I can
say about the likewise the London-based Muslim Institute. It
was in particular Samia Rahman of the Muslim Institute who
has always encouraged me to write and who has also become a
very dear friend. Farouk Peru, it was you who introduced me to
the Muslim Institute. I will always be thankful for that and I
miss our long discussions. What has sustained me more than
anything on my journey with Islam and with this book is my
beloved circle of friends. Among them in particular, in the UK,
Sahil Warsi, Arthur Dudney, Hannaan Baig and Tawseef Khan.
Ibrahim Subdurally and Ameet Shah, I miss our annual meet-up
traditions, Covid and Brexit have forced a bit of a break on them.
In the USA or Turkey or Spain (or wherever you may be when
you read this): Logan Sparks, uncountable blessings reached my
life just through you. In Germany, my first and foremost thanks
go to the wonderful Rita Sonal Panjatan and Danijel Cubelic.
And also to Ali Raza and Rzouga Selmi. Antony Pattathu, so
many thanks for dragging me out into the sunlight when I
needed it most. Saboura Naqshband, I really wish Rita and you
were closer, our slumber-parties always give me life. The man in

ACKNOWLEDGEMENTS

my life, my wonderful partner Asim, has not only constantly nourished me with his love, but has also always encouraged me in believing in myself and in my ability to complete this project. Many others have contributed to this book: Ali Ghandour, many thanks for your own wonderful work on sexuality and Islam and for a couple of wonderful discussions with you. Omar Kasmani, thank you for a few significant anthropological insights that I would have missed out on without you. Oliver Kontny, thank you for sharing my love of the apocalypse and for having given me very tangible help in times of need. Samira, thank you for your insight into modern Omani society. Dear Paula Schrode, parts of this book were once meant to become a PhD thesis under your supervision. Life took some other turns. But your support and help at Bayreuth University has played an important role in getting me to the point of writing this story down and I still keep telling people that you are the most wonderful boss that I ever had. Last but definitely not least a big thank you goes out to the wonderful people at Hurst who have helped me enormously in turning the vision of this book into a tangible fact. Especially to Farhaana Arefin who has supported me in this project for over a year and to Lara Weisweiller-Wu who helped me bring it to completion, and to their wonderful team of copy editors.

GLOSSARY

Badhai   Derived from a Hindi word meaning 'congratulating', *badhai* is the practice through which *hijras* offer blessings at weddings and births, usually in exchange for donations to the *gharana* (see below). *Hijras* go out on *badhai* on days considered auspicious, performing songs, dances and prayers for newlyweds and the families of new-born children in their neighbourhood.

Chela   The younger, or more junior, initiates into *hijra gharanas*. On initiation, each *chela* develops a mentorship bond with an elder, or more senior, *hijra*, known as a guru, and is considered their initiatory 'child'. *Chelas* are often the bread-winners of the *gharana*, and are usually those who go out on *badhai*.

Dera   A communal house in which *hijras* live, derived from the Hindi/Urdu word meaning 'camp'.

Gharana   A family, clan or community into which *hijras* are initiated. The word *gharana* is related to the Hindi/Urdu word *'ghar'*, meaning house. Although members of a *gharana* are not related by blood, there is usually a hierarchical, kinship structure within the 'family'. *Chelas* who share a bond with a particular guru may refer to each other as *guru bhai* (guru brothers) or *behen* (sister), while the guru of a *hijra*'s guru is known as a *daadi guru* (grandmother guru).

PREFACE

THIS IS A BOOK for the uprooted, the in-betweens, the mixed and the misfits. As such, it is a book for everybody, as we live in a world in which more and more people feel a sense of uprooted-ness, of not fitting in and of drawing inspiration and identity from a wide range of sources. We all exist in plural and diverse societies, and we all struggle with how that plurality and diversity relates to us personally and how we can manage it in our lives. This has occurred, strangely, while as human beings we have also all become more similar to each other than ever before in history. Genders have become more alike in terms of rights and agency, and cultures have become increasingly hybridised and globalised.

The few very marked differences that remain we find unbear-able to deal with, and so we retreat to increasingly simplified ideas about who we are and how we differ from others. The rise of the alt-right, Islamism, Islamophobia, Hindutva, Brexit, men's rights movements, straight pride, trans exclusionary radical femin-ism and other similar visions seems to be rooted in this. As are many of the progressive and liberal replies to these ideological challenges, unfortunately. In many ways, this book is meant to testify against these kinds of myopic visions and to present a more complicated, but at the same time, much more enjoyable and optimistic analysis of identity. I hope I have succeeded.

PREFACE

I am deliberately vague here in saying what this book is about. But this is because a lot of what I have to say will remain vague. Not in the sense of obscurantism, but rather in the sense of ambivalence and ambiguity. I do not want to provide clear answers to issues of identity; I want to keep open a discussion that far too many people see in dogmatic and orthodox terms. Identity is always fragile, it is always vulnerable, and it is always ambiguous. But, and that is one of the main theses of my book, that is precisely where the true strength of identity lies.

Having said that, I am still in the realm of vagueness. The reader who has bought this book, has seen the cover and read the blurb may be becoming somewhat impatient with me at this stage. They will want to know when I am going to start talking about eunuchs and *hijras* and transgender people.

I will get onto this. But let me first clear up a misconception that some readers may have: this is not a book about the *hijra* or *khwajasara* community as such, and it is certainly not a book that attempts to speak for it. The community has been subject to much academic research and media inquiries, and in many cases, it has seen itself misrepresented and abused as a result. Writing about the 'other' is always a tricky issue, whether from an academic or journalistic perspective. Too often it leads to the 'other' being seen through a colonial prism, subjecting it to a kind of epistemic rape. I am an anthropologist by training and at some point in my life this book, or at least parts of it, was supposed to become my PhD thesis in Religious Studies. But I felt that the academic discourse was too often forcing me into insincerity. The anthropological experience is a subjective one, and it changes you as much as it changes the 'other' you encounter. But in academia, we play at being objective observers, at being analysts, at being teachers. Far less often do we speak about being someone who had to learn, someone who was changed or someone who cannot emotionally disentangle themselves from their experiences.

PREFACE

Why did I become an anthropologist in the first place? I was about 16 years old when I discovered the work of Bengali film-maker Satyajit Ray. The first Ray movie I ever watched was *Agantuk* (*The Stranger*, 1991), which was actually the last he directed. It was an underrated meditation on the question of 'identity', both individual and social. It was probably this movie that introduced the word 'anthropologist' to me for the first time, suggesting an academic career to me that I would later try to pursue. Of course, the movie's idea of what an anthropologist is and does is quite different from academic anthropology, as I would later discover.

The movie did, however, foreshadow another experience I would later have. The central character of *Agantuk* is a man who ventures out into the world and disappears for many years. When he returns to his home in Kolkata, he has become completely unrecognisable to his own people. His long absence and his relatives' doubts regarding his identity is the more apparent explanation for his unrecognisability. But there is also a subtext that tells us that it is encountering the world itself that changes us into someone else. The stranger eventually manages to reconnect with his family when he himself recognises a desire to explore and discover the world first in his grand-nephew and later in his niece. In one particular scene of the movie, the stranger tells his grand-nephew to never become a '*kupa munduk*', an Adivasi term for a frog sitting at the bottom of the well, unaware of what lies beyond his limited and dark horizon.

Ever since I watched that movie the phrase *kupa munduk* has stayed with me. I started to understand my sense of alienation and not-belonging in the world in which I grew up in relation to that term. I understood that I was not meant to be a *kupa munduk*. I could not answer all the questions that I had on identity and belonging by remaining in my dark little well. I had to see and experience other worlds. It seemed to me that the world around me was composed of and ruled by *kupa munduks*.

PREFACE

Watched a few decades later, Satyajit Ray's film is not without flaws. It centres on the anxieties of upper-middle-class Indians to not become *kupa munduks*. Servants working in the homes of those upper-middle-class families and the featured Adivasi people largely remain without a voice. But that in itself also highlights a crucial aspect of trying to escape the *kupa munduks* of this world. Marginalised communities are rarely imagined to be taking part in that venture. (Words like 'cosmopolitan' or 'global citizen' themselves evoke images of affluent international jet-setters.) They are the studied 'other'. But they are not imagined as active teachers.

Why did I feel a sense of alienation and not-belonging to this world and why did I need to escape the *kupa munduks*? I grew up in a small town in Germany. From an early age it became clear to me that two defining factors would always play a huge role in my life: my Muslim faith and my transgender identity. Negotiating the demands of these two sides of my personality was not always easy within the conservative and provincial environment in which I grew up, nor was it in the conservative Muslim diaspora communities that framed my life.

My struggle with this eventually led me to become a cultural anthropologist and a scholar of religion. But, even more significantly, it led me to India and Pakistan, where I spent the most formative period of my life in a 'third-gender' community. The members of this community are known as *hijras* in India. In Pakistan the same word is known too, but in recent years it has given way to the more politically correct term *khwajasara*. In the pre-colonial past, these *hijras/khwajasaras* worked as eunuchs in the harems and palaces of the Muslim aristocracy and held important positions in the Mughal Empire and in the Princely States. Traditionally, both Muslim and Hindu communities in South Asia have believed that the third gender has special powers to bless or to curse others. As such, *hijras/khwajasaras* had always been highly respected as agents of the spiritual and supernatural.

But under British colonial rule, they were persecuted and became an increasingly marginalised community. Now, in independent India and Pakistan, this community has started to fight for its rights. Especially in Pakistan, their struggle has been an amazing success story: in 2009, the Pakistani Supreme Court officially introduced a 'third gender' to the nation's bureaucracy, and since 2018 a special anti-discrimination law for the 'third gender' has been in place. The community has also, for many years now, increasingly engaged with global discourses on gender and sexuality.

I encountered the *hijra/khwajasara* community for the first time in India in the early 2000s and since then, two decades on, it has been an integral part of my life. It has shaped my view on gender and sexuality. It has helped me understand the relationship between being a trans woman and being a Muslim in my own society in a new light. It has made me question the ways we often discuss issues of belonging and identity.

I do not want to speak for this community. But I want to speak about my own encounter with it. And I want to write about what such an encounter has to say about the world we live in and its obsession with difference and identity. My experience may be seen as very specific, exceptional, 'exotic'. But I believe that it is actually very emblematic for our times, in which more and more people—despite myopic policies and increasingly parochial ideologies—experience themselves as having several cultural roots, have links across borders, and find themselves juggling many different identities at once. I also believe that for all of us, gender and sexuality are important parts of who and what we are, and that on some level we all struggle to reconcile these different parts. Looking at the diversity of human cultures therefore allows us to speak to everybody and gives us important insights into ourselves and our place in this world.

I wrote this book in the years 2020 and 2021, a troubling period for a lot of people, but particularly troubling for the subject matter of this work. In the UK and in Germany, these years saw a particularly ugly debate between representatives of different branches of feminism: one which holds that transgender women are in fact men and should therefore not be allowed in women's spaces (including public bathrooms), and another, more inclusive feminism, which maintains that different experiences of being a woman are possible and that feminism can only fulfil its role if it represents all women—including transgender women. At the same time, our whole planet was struck by the Covid-19 pandemic, and it quickly became clear that transgender people still constitute some of the most marginalised communities globally, deeply affected by structural issues. This is an aspect that has been completely missing from most of the heated debates on transgender issues in the West. The pandemic left many transgender women in South Asia in particular in desperate situations in which they had no access to income and were often denied proper medical care. But this situation also proved the great resilience of transgender communities. In India as much as in Pakistan, transgender women often self-organised to give aid not only to their own communities but to their neighbourhoods too.

In a tragic way, these years gave me an opportunity to reflect on the place of transgender identities in societies, and on the power of marginalised communities playing an active role in our world. The reflections inspired by the specific struggles of our time have come together with several other experiences I have had over the past few years. This has been just as much in my capacity as a private person with a very specific individual experience in this world, as in my identity as a Muslim believer and as an academic trained in Cultural Anthropology and secular Religious Studies. I bring together these experiences and reflections here and hope that I have succeeded in turning them into a kaleidoscope through which the reader can look at the realities of sex, gender, faith, identity and belonging in new colours.

PREFACE

A few last notes related to the language of this book:

It has become a common cliché to call all kinds of traditional South Asian transgender or third-gender people '*hijras*'. This is a mistake. There have always been several different gender-variant communities and identities in South Asia, some tied to specific regions, some more to class. Many of them do overlap with each other, however. In its strictest sense, the *hijra/khwajasara* community is a very specific cultural category and tradition, among many others. But nowadays, due to the media, globalisation and the influence of embassies and international NGOs, all of these categories are increasingly understood under the umbrella of 'transgender identity', and several *hijras*, *khwajasaras* and members of other South Asian communities have started to identify themselves as 'transgender' or even 'transgender women' now.

The title of this book may confuse some, or even offend. Eunuchs? Transgender? Is it correct to conflate these categories? Throughout this book, I embark upon a journey of exploration of these and other historical and cultural categories. Whether *hijras* in India, *khwajasaras* in Pakistan and other traditional third-gender concepts can be identified with modern transgender women in the West is an old anthropological question. As is the question of whether historical categories such as 'eunuchs' matter in that context. Is 'being transgender' a universal experience that occurs in all cultures and societies but is just labelled differently? Or are such categories culturally contingent and tied to their social context? I will touch on these questions in the book. But more precisely, I ask: How is the experience of these categories impacted when one belongs to or moves between several social and cultural contexts? Because in our day and age, an increasing number of people, myself included, do precisely that.

I write about my experience as a transgender woman who has lived and moved in *hijra* and *khwajasara* spaces. As such I mostly write about transfeminine experiences and transfeminine communities. A whole other book could be written about the meaning of transmasculine experiences in South Asia and in Muslim contexts, but that is not a task for me. I do think, however, that a lot of my reflections are not only relevant to the experiences of transfeminine people, but are also reflections on the larger cultural, social and religious nature of gender. At the end of the day, that nature affects all of us, whether we are transfeminine or transmasculine, cis or trans, queer or straight, men, women or other.

My transcription of Hindi, Urdu, Persian and Arabic words is not always fully consistent and does not obey academic standards. I sometimes employ a free transliteration that the reader may know from Bollywood film titles, song lyrics and social media. This is the language of our global reality, a language that is perpetually changing, developing and following sometimes opposing rules inspired by differing sources. In that sense, it is the language that also best represents this story.

INTRODUCTION

LIFE IN THE HOUSE

WHEN I THINK OF the first time I stayed in a *hijra* house, in Delhi for a few months in the early 2000s, there is one image that immediately springs to mind. I think it may have clung to my memory in especially vivid colours because it surprised me so much, particularly after all of my experiences in my little German mosque community.

The house I was staying in at that time was in a part of New Delhi that had originally been a small village, before being swallowed up by the maw of the Indian capital. A wilder and more vibrant New Delhi was bustling just a few streets away, but here, in our house and its immediate neighbourhood, it still felt very much like village life. The house had many floors and a flat roof, as is common in South Asia. In front of the house was a little square that had once marked something like the centre of the village. And right across from the entrance to our house was the little Friday mosque.

The image in my mind, the one that has imprinted itself so firmly on my memory, is of the other girls and me sitting on the stairs of one of the upper floors of our house, putting on make-up and jewellery and getting ready for the day. Right across from us, on the upper floor of the mosque, was a class of teenage boys memorising the recitation of the Holy Quran, all dressed impeccably in white *shalwar kameez*, the typical dress of *madrasa* boys in South Asia. Some of the girls were roughly the same age as the boys on the other side and, as we applied our make-up, would sneak occasional glances over at the boys. Sometimes, one or two of the boys would glance back over at us. There were smiles and suppressed laughter on both sides and, at times, small signs of flirtation.

From time to time, the teacher would notice what was going on and tell his students not to pay so much attention to the *hijras* on the other side. The situation was further complicated by my presence, that of a European foreigner, which provoked a particular inquisitiveness amongst the boys. Occasionally, one of the older *hijras* noticed and told the girls not to glance over too provocatively. Once or twice, they asked me to sit in some spot where I would not be so easily exposed to the boys' glances. But there was never any genuine tension or discomfort in the air. The *madrasa* students and the pious Quran teacher on the other side were quite used to having a bunch of glamorous third-gender ladies as neighbours, and the *hijras* themselves found nothing unusual in living right next to a mosque. In fact, even in the grand old parts of Old Delhi or Lahore, it was very common to find some of the best-known *hijra* homes in close proximity to the large Mughal-built Friday mosques.

I have just referred to the place we lived in as a 'house' and 'home', but I should be a bit clearer here. The community of *hijras* and *khwajasaras* is organised into several lines that can be described as huge clans or families, although the members of these families are not related by blood, merely initiation into the same artistic 'school'. In Hindi and Urdu, these lines are usually referred to as *gharanas*, a word also used in other contexts. The lineages linking classical Indian music and dance artists by apprenticeship or style are usually referred to as *gharanas*, for example. Ultimately, this word is related to '*ghar*', which simply means house in Hindi and Urdu. It has, therefore, become common to refer to these initiatory families as 'houses'. There is a special beauty in this translation, because it recalls, for me, the 'houses' of New York City's ballroom culture, inhabited by transgender and genderqueer people of colour, and most famously depicted in the documentary *Paris is Burning* (1990) and US drama series *Pose* (2018–2021). Not ignoring the fact that these communities are separated by oceans, cultures and very different paths of history, both subcultures consist of surrogate families headed by elders who teach younger members of the community, usually from lower-income and socially marginalised groups, about a way of living.

These initiatory houses or *gharanas*, however, are not identical with the places that *hijras* live in. The *hijras* that belong to a specific *gharana* are often spread all over cities, regions and countries and may live in several places. Some *hijras* who can afford to do so may live in their own apartments; some live with their families or romantic partners. But many, especially those who cannot afford any other home or who have been thrown out by their birth families, live in homes such as the house across from the mosque, together with other members of their lineage. In fact, this is the experience of most *hijras*. These communal houses that *hijras* live in are called *dera*, a Hindi/Urdu word meaning 'camp', often used for the settlements of Hindu or Muslim religious mendicants. These two words, *gharana* and *dera*, actually tell us a lot about the traditional self-image of the *hijra* and *khwajasara* community. On the one hand, this is a community related to the same vanished world of royal courts and aristocratic patronisation that musicians and dancers once used to inhabit and, in fact, the *hijras* are often good musicians and dancers in their own right. On the other hand, the community has also always understood itself as a spiritual community as well and not a few *hijras* understand themselves as a kind of dervish.

Both within the *gharana* and within the *dera*, life is organised according to an implicit hierarchy that traditionally structures all of *hijra* life. I have written above that a *gharana* functions like a family or a clan and for those young *hijras* in particular who have been thrown out and deserted by their birth families, the *gharana* often does function as a surrogate family. Families in South Asia are traditionally often organised according to strict patriarchal principles and the *hijra gharana* is no exception—although the word 'patriarchal' may be a bit confusing in this context since we are not speaking about people who identify as men or as fathers. The elders of the community are those who have the most privilege and also have the most agency to make decisions for the community. However, being an 'elder' is not necessarily tied to the actual age of the community member but is rather a matter of one's place in the initiatory line; the further up you are in the line, the more power and influence you usually have.

These influential people are usually older than those further down the initiatory line, but they do not have to be. Elders are usually referred to as 'guru' in the community. The guru of your guru would be your *daadi guru* (grandmother guru). The highest and most senior guru, the leader of the *gharana*, is often referred to as the *naayak*. When you and another *hijra* share an initiatory bond with a particular guru, then you two are *guru bhai* (guru brothers). You may also call your *guru bhai* your *behen*, your sister. In fact, all *hijras* of a similar initiatory rank as you would be called your sisters. These words display a creative use of gendered nouns that is very characteristic of the language spoken within the community. A guru may also function as your 'mother', although it is common to keep these roles apart as many prefer to consider another elder, who is not their immediate guru, their 'mother'. In fact, something that is often overlooked by researchers, writers and even local South Asian transgender activists is that these categories do not always relate to each other in the same way depending on the locations in which they are employed. *Hijras* of different *gharanas*, *deras* and also different regions and cities sometimes understand these categories in different ways.

One becomes a member of a *gharana* through initiation and only after such initiation can you be considered a real *hijra* or

khwajasara. Being born with a specific nature is the one require-
ment to become suitable for initiation, so, in one sense, one is
indeed always 'born as a *hijra*'. But just as in a traditional patriarchal understanding—where womanhood remains suspect until
confirmed by marriage—a *hijra* is only considered a real *hijra*
once she has undergone initiation. In many South Asian societies, marriage is, for a woman, traditionally understood as an act
of transition from her family household of birth to her husband's
family household. The initiation of a *hijra* is likewise understood
as such an act of transition. With this initiation, the *hijra* ritually
leaves her original caste and family—although, in reality, she will
often still maintain a loving connection with them if they allow
her to do so—and becomes part of a lineage that leads far back
into ancient times.

In the case of my own *dera*, the line of the *gharana* is said to
lead back directly to the court eunuchs of the Mughal palaces.
The ritual of initiation itself is characterised by a lot of symbolism that can be found in South Asian marriage ceremonies.
There is a *mehndi* (henna) ceremony and the newly initiated *chela*
receives a red bridal *dupatta*. The *chela* is thereby bound to the
gharana and to her guru. Contrary to what the South Asian
yellow press has claimed, there is no sexual or romantic element
to this ritual. It merely serves the purpose of making the *chela*
part of a new family system.

As with any family system, this system can be exploited in
harmful ways, but it can also work as a haven of love and support
for its members. While I have seen examples of *gharanas* and
deras devolving into the quasi-mafia-like structures they are
often rumoured to be in South Asian mainstream society, I have
known far more cases of *hijras* experiencing their *gharana* and
dera as a true family which has given them the support their
birth family was never willing to give them. Just as there can be
abusive fathers and mothers, there can also be abusive gurus.

Conversely, just as there are excellent fathers and mothers, there are also excellent gurus. Economic circumstances often have an influence on these issues. Difficult economic circumstances create more pressure and, just as in birth families, the more pressure there is, the greater the likelihood of violence and abuse within the family. I have also observed that the bigger a *gharana* becomes and the less immediate the relationships between its members are, the more the relationships become about money and not so much about personal support.

In any case, there is a mutual dependency between the gurus and their initiatory children, who are called *chela*. The *chelas* are usually the actual bread-winners of the family. They are often those *hijras* and *khwajasaras* you will see at traffic lights and crossroads and on trains and buses in cities, asking those who pass by for money in exchange for a prayer or blessing—'begging' is the wrong word here because, at least according to traditional understanding, the giver of money does indeed receive something in return. In the more prestigious *gharanas*, most *chelas* do not engage in these kind of activities. Instead, they leave the house in groups almost every morning to perform songs and dances at the houses of bridal couples or new-born male children and to bless the respective couple or new-born child. Traditionally, these blessings of couples and children used to form the largest part of the income of a *dera*. Many *hijras* also engage in sex work, although it differs from *gharana* to *gharana* whether this is done with the explicit knowledge or feigned ignorance of the gurus. I have heard many gurus, including the gurus of my own house, claim that sex work goes against the principles of the community. As in many human communities, the ideal often diverges from the practice.

The money earned by the *chelas* is usually given to the senior guru of the *dera* and sometimes also to a council of senior gurus. The council then decide for which purposes the earned money will be used. The *chelas* always receive a set portion of the money to spend according to their own wishes. Another portion is used to make sure there is always enough food in the *dera* and that all the *chelas* are well dressed. The gurus often keep larger amounts of money for their own needs, but this is generally understood as a practice appropriate to their status. I have rarely seen a guru revel in luxury, while her *chelas* lived in poverty. For many gurus it is a matter of personal pride to make sure that their *chelas* tell others that their guru is a good and caring guru. In return, the gurus do not only provide food and clothes but also give the *chelas* an infrastructure of support in life that they can always rely on.

The gurus teach the *chelas* music and dance, about the history and customs of the community and give them advice on multiple topics. The gurus can also discipline misbehaving *chelas*. Stories of abusive gurus who misuse their right to discipline their *chelas* come to the surface regularly, although a guru who disciplines her *chelas* too often and too harshly will not usually make a good name for herself within the community. It is also not uncommon for a *chela* to flee an abusive guru or *dera* and seek refuge with a new guru. According to the rules of the *hijra* community, the new guru then usually has to reimburse the old guru for the loss of a 'bread-winner', but I have also heard of cases in which a guru had created such a bad reputation for herself that it was she who was chastised by the community and had to pay a fine.

As I found out after my stay in the *dera* across from the little mosque, these hierarchies and rules all function in pretty much the same way across North India, Pakistan and Bangladesh— though, as I have pointed out, there can be slightly differing local customs and understandings of categories. There are also regular gatherings at which the different *gharanas* present in a specific city or region interact with each other and discuss how to deal with issues such as the transfer of a *chela* from one guru to the other (which does not have to be tied to instances of abuse; in most cases *hijras* change gurus for much more harmless reasons).

Likewise, very much the same across all borders is the intra-community language that is spoken by *hijras* and *khwajasaras*: *farsi*. The word literally means 'Persian', but in this case it refers to a secret vocabulary that has nothing to do with the official language of Iran (though the name may have something to do with the use of Persian at the royal courts of Muslim rulers of the past). In Pakistan, this *farsi* is usually spoken in conjunction with a Punjabi syntax, grammar and additional vocabulary. In Northern India and Hyderabad, Urdu is usually the language that gives it its outer form; in Bangladesh and West Bengal it is often Bengali. The basic vocabulary of this *farsi* always remains the same across these languages, however, and as such must have its roots in pre-Partition India, if not even earlier.

Hijras are not the only people in South Asia to employ such a private 'language'. In fact, a lot of marginalised groups and castes in South Asia have their own vocabularies unknown to outsiders. Such group vocabularies or dialects are meant to make communication possible without outsiders to the community understanding. What is quite interesting, however, is that in more recent times, parts of the *hijra farsi* has also been adopted by modern gay and queer communities in India and Pakistan. In recent years, some of the *farsi* vocabulary has even seeped into mainstream society, through the depiction of *khwajasara*, transgender and gay culture in Pakistani and Indian movies and drama series. The brilliant Pakistani comedy series *Quddusi Sahab Ki Bewah* (2012–2014) for example, has made copious use of *farsi*.

What has changed over the decades, is the way in which members of the community want to be addressed in the public sphere. This has not remained the same in India and Pakistan; the word *hijra* still remains fairly common and is understood as a neutral term in India today, but in Pakistan it has increasingly become understood as an insult in recent decades. Members of the Pakistani community are now officially referred to as *khwa-*

jasara in Urdu, a word which originally designated a court eunuch. The word is also commonly used with Punjabified spellings and pronunciations, such as '*Khwaja Sira*'. The original Punjabi word for *hijra*, *khusra* (probably a derivative of *khwajasara*), is in Pakistan now also generally understood to be an insult, although it is often used in a neutral way in rural areas and was used as a self-designation until the early 2000s. In India, one can nowadays sometimes find the word *kinnar* being used instead of *hijra*. This word seems to intentionally tie the community to a pre-Muslim Hindu mythology (*kinnars* are the musicians of the Hindu gods, hybrid bird-human beings). It is due to these differences that in this book I sometimes speak of *hijras*, sometimes of *khwajasaras* and sometimes both, even though the community is essentially the same. I try to use *khwajasara* specifically when speaking about the Pakistani contexts and *hijra* when addressing the Indian context, but in other cases I do not favour one over the other.

What has also changed with time, in both India and Pakistan, is how *hijras* and *khwajasaras* are conceptualised in the eyes of mainstream society. Most *khwajasaras* can easily be identified as what we in the West would call a 'transgender woman'. That means, they have been assigned the male gender at birth and were often raised as boys, but very early in life they identified as feminine and later preferred to behave and dress in a feminine way. They are also usually attracted sexually and romantically to men, which is not always the case for Western transgender women nowadays, who often identify as lesbian or bisexual women. Traditionally, *khwajasaras* would often undergo a ceremony of ritual castration that would render their bodies more feminine and was understood as a religious sacrifice. Many *khwajasaras* and *hijras* are not transgender, however, but are intersex. Many others do not neatly fit into transgender or intersex categories but may identify as *khwajasara* because they feel that they fall outside of the usual gender binary in other ways.

All of these diverse people were once able to find their place within the community, where these differences have never mattered as much as they did to the outside world. What mattered was mostly whether one had been legitimately initiated or not. Since colonial times, South Asian mainstream society has been preoccupied with the idea that there are 'real *khwajasaras*' and 'fake *khwajasaras*' (understood to be men posing as *hijras*). This preoccupation has often led to an obsession with the bodies of *khwajasaras*. I remember that in the 1990s and early 2000s, *hijras* in India only very rarely used the category 'transgender' to identify themselves. They were keen, however, to stress in public that they were either intersex or castrated, to dispel any notion that they may be 'fake'.

In the time between my first interactions with the Delhi *hijra* community and the publication of this book, the self-image of the community has changed considerably. In the last decade, the vast majority of *khwajasara* and *hijra* activists in India and Pakistan have started to identify as 'transgender' and also increasingly as 'transgender women'. In Pakistan in particular, the word *khwajasara* is now often understood as a direct translation of 'transgender' and news outlets even use it for transgender men, who traditionally have never been a part of the *khwajasara* community. On the other hand, some activists are now alleging that the general South Asian public confuses transgender people with intersex people.

While some younger members of the *khwajasara* and *hijra* community now identify with modern Western ideas of gender and want to be seen as transgender women, during my early days in the community, such notions were virtually unknown. There were many *hijras* who understood themselves as having a 'feminine soul' (*zanana ruh*) but whenever I told them that many transgender women in the West want to be seen as real women, they found the idea ridiculous. The *hijras* that I had met back then were very proud of their special status. A status that, on the one hand, connected them to a long history of royal and sacred eunuchs both in Hinduism and Islam and that, on the other hand, gave them spiritual powers that no cisgender woman could ever possess.

It was precisely because *hijras* fell outside of the gender binary, were often rejected by their birth family and could never lead the life of a traditional South Asian cisgender heterosexual woman, that the Divine had given them the power to bless and curse others, in particular in all matters related to romance, sexuality and procreation. The *hijras* back then may sometimes have envied cisgender heterosexual women for being able to lead a regular married life and for giving birth to children—in fact, infertile women who were not able to give birth to children were sometimes also understood as a type of *hijra* by them—but they were very clear that they themselves did not identify as women and also did not want to be identified as women.

In the early 2000s in Delhi, we would leave the house in little groups almost every day—except on Fridays, holidays and days that were deemed astrologically unlucky—to do a work that was usually called *badhai*: a Hindi word that literally means 'congratulating'. Each group had a leader that kept notes of the houses in the larger neighbourhood in which a wedding had taken place recently or a male child given birth to. It is often said that *hijras* employ a complex system of espionage to gather information on such events, but the truth is that it is not difficult to get such information in South Asia, where weddings and child births are talked about all the time. In those days at least, it was not uncommon for families to directly invite the *hijras*, because there were still many people in mainstream society who genuinely believed in the sacred powers of *hijras*. It was always very important to invite the right *hijras* because different *gharanas* had different territories to do their *badhai*-work, territories that hailed back to privileges given in Mughal times.

We always visited a few families every day, demonstrating the breadth of our *gharana*'s territory. There was never a day without a childbirth or wedding, even during seasons which were not typically considered wedding seasons. When our group knocked at a family's door, a ritualised exchange ensued. In cases where the family itself had invited us, we were usually let into the apartment or home immediately. In other cases, it sometimes took a bit of persuasion from the leader of our group. In fact, such persuasion is also quite often ritualised; in many neighbourhoods families do not want to give the impression that they would let *hijras* in too easily and so, in order to preserve the honour of these respective families, *hijras* often act as if they are forcing their way in. The truth is that the families we visited always seemed entertained by our presence and enjoyed it a lot, even more so since our group unusually contained a European *hijra*. The attitude that many people had towards *hijras*, at least at that time, was a strange mix of religious reverence, superstitious fear and unease in the presence of an unknown sexuality.

Our group was always accompanied by a hired professional player of a *dholak* drum. Subsequently, in Pakistan, I saw it was far more common for *khwajasaras* themselves to play the *dholak*, but our *gharana* was quite proud of the fact we were able to hire someone to do the job for us. Sometimes the *dholak* player was accompanied by a harmonium player. More than once I felt quite charmed by these men and their presence in our group could be quite disruptive at times, I have to admit. There was never time to discuss much beyond work with them though, as we spent very busy days together, walking to the point of exhaustion through the Indian heat from house to house, singing and dancing at every stop. There is a very characteristic clap that only *hijras* do and that sounds a bit like two halves of a coconut shell struck against each other. It is this rhythmic clap that announces the arrival of a group of *hijras* to a neighbourhood and it is with this clap that *hijras* accompany the songs they sing once they are let into the home of a family.

The first songs to be sung are usually the most recent Bollywood hits, to which *hijras* dance while trying to copy the accompanying movie choreographies. In the past, *hijras* would have sung more poetic and classical pieces and would have danced the *mujra* dance of the courtesans. A song or two with religious significance would be included, either a Hindu *bhajan* or a song in praise of a Muslim sufi saint. Then the present bridal couple or new-born child would be blessed. The respective family always had to bring out a quantity of sugar, flour and rice, which was used for the blessing and taken home by the group afterwards. The blessing of a bridal couple was always supposed to make sure that the couple would live in happiness and produce many healthy children. The blessing of the new-born male child, on the other hand, was always accompanied by the leader of our group holding up the child and quickly inspecting his genitalia to confirm to the parents that the child was not intersex and would not become 'like us'.

When the blessings were finished, a negotiation for the amount of money to be given by the family began. This negotiation, led by the leader of our group, was usually accompanied by a lot of bawdy jokes and vigorous clapping. If a family did not agree quickly enough to give the amount of money desired, the clapping would become especially aggressive and the leader would remind the family that we could curse them instead of blessing them. A particularly feared threat was the warning that we would undress and expose our genitals if we were not paid properly. In fact, the sight of the genitals of an intersex or castrated *hijra* was traditionally understood as something like a 'Medusa's gaze' that could call down all kinds of calamities. I never witnessed any one of us actually exposing our genitals, however, as it never came to that point. As in the case of the ritualised entrance, these negotiations were usually more to pro-tect the honour of the family than anything else. There was rarely any genuine opposition to paying us for the diversion, entertainment and blessing we had given.

At the time of my earliest stays in the community, however, my sisters had already started to complain that fewer and fewer families would directly invite them and that there had even been families that started to chase them away when they approached. Threatening them with curses did not help because, apparently, these people did not believe in *hijras'* powers anymore. They con-sidered *hijras* an embarrassment to Indian culture. Indian Hindus had increasingly started to blame the existence of this embarrass-ment on Muslims—they had, after all, invented all this court eunuch and castration business, it was said—while Pakistani Muslims sometimes claimed that it was the negative influence of Hindu culture that had created this social phenomenon (what else, they thought, could be the origin of all these strange ideas about curses and blessings? Certainly not the Quran). A success-ful Indian and Pakistani transgender activism would only take off properly ten years later.

For the community, both in India and Pakistan, things, there-fore, looked quite bleak. In the West, at that time, transgender issues did not have the attention that they have now and the Western-centric global LGBT movement was strongly domi-nated by the 'G'. A number of gay NGOs had appeared in both India and Pakistan at that time that seemed to have very little awareness of transgender or *hijra* issues. I personally witnessed members of these NGOs approaching *hijras* and telling them that they were just confused gay men. There was a lot of money and a lot of epistemic power behind those NGOs, even though the gay men who organised them faced their own issues of mar-ginalisation and discrimination in South Asian societies.

The presence of the NGOs made quite an impression both on the *hijra* community and mainstream society. One time we were visiting a family and suddenly a member of that family started to insult us as 'homos'. The incident itself was very shocking but what shocked me even more was that afterwards a sister approached me and asked, 'Is it true? We are homos?' She was under the impression that there must be something to all these fancy theories that were preached by Westerners and modern upper-middle-class Indians alike. It seemed quite attractive to her that many people in India who did identify as 'homo' or 'gay' led relatively comfortable, privileged lives and did not have to obey any guru. What occupied her most, however, was the idea that if more and more people started to regard *hijras* as just that, either 'homosexual men who dress up as women' or 'transgender women who were real women in the wrong body' (as I had told her many people in the West understood themselves), then her community would lose its special meaning in culture and society. She seemed torn between both the positive and the negative potential that such a development could bring.

For the time being, *hijras* still had a special meaning in culture and society, however—at least to some people. Our *dera* could still comfortably get by just on the earnings we collected every day from blessing brides and babies. Such was our regular routine, day-in and day-out, house after house. We returned to our *dera* in the afternoon, utterly exhausted from all of the walking, dancing, clapping and arguing. The money earned was given to the gurus. We ate and we rested. In the evenings some of us would clandestinely sneak out for another kind of work or sometimes to meet an actual romantic interest, perhaps one of the boys from the *madrasa* on the other side of the village square. But most of us would be far too tired to do so. Romance and love were saved for holidays. We had a late dinner, then we slept, in order to get up again the next morning. To get dressed again and do our make-up while being observed by the *madrasa* boys. To again venture out into a busy day.

1

A TRANSNATIONAL JOURNEY

HOW DID I END up there in 2000, a European Muslim transgender woman in the *dera* across from the mosque? Dancing, clapping and blessing in Delhi? Beginning a journey that had led me to further explore *hijra* and *khwajasara* communities in India and Pakistan and that had eventually also brought me to understand much more about who I am?

I do, in fact, believe that we cannot reach an understanding of our own selves unless we explore the world around us. I believe that very much as a Muslim as well, for in the Holy Quran God tells us: 'We will show them Our signs in the horizons and in themselves, 'til it is clear to them that this is the truth' [41:53]. The Quran also teaches us: 'We created you male and female, and We made you into various nations and tribes, so that you may know each other' [49:13]. The Prophet Muhammad, peace be upon him and on his family, has taught us: 'Search for knowledge, even if you have to travel as far as China for it.' And one of the most revered figures of Islam, the Prophet's son-in-law Imam 'Ali ibn Abi Talib, reportedly once said that a person who has never travelled is like an arrow that has never left its bow.

In our world of borders and nation states the importance that travelling once held for the spiritual, cultural and economic development of the Islamic world is unfortunately often forgotten today. It still remains visible in one of the most fundamental pillars of Islam, the Hajj, the pilgrimage to Makkah. This pillar asks every Muslim who can afford to, at least once in their lifetime, to leave the comfort of their home and travel across the world to the centre of Islam, thereby also encountering countless other Muslims from all continents and corners of the world.

Being able to go on this pilgrimage has always been somewhat of a privilege, of course, and being able to travel has become even more of a privilege in these times. Nevertheless, countless Muslims with lesser means have undertaken that journey throughout the centuries, experiencing a large number of different cultures and contexts. This has contributed to the essentially cosmopolitan character of Muslim societies all over the world for centuries.

Beyond the Hajj, classical Islam also celebrated the scholarly ideal of the *rihla 'ilmiyya*, the journey in search of knowledge. The precedent for this journey was set by the Prophet Muhammad himself (p.b.u.h.), who in his youth had been accompanying caravans travelling all across the Arab desert, from Yemen to Syria. The *rihla 'ilmiyya* was put into practice by almost every major intellectual figure of Muslim history and, in fact, one was not really taken seriously as a Muslim scholar if one had not left home in search of knowledge at least once. We may here mention Ghazali's journeys between Central Asia and Egypt or Ibn 'Arabi's journey, taking him from his native Spain to today's Turkey and finally leading him to settle down in Syria. Most famous of all is the Moroccan Ibn Battuta, of course, who traversed the larger part of Eurasia in the fourteenth century, recording eyewitness accounts from places as far apart from each other as European Russia, China and the Maldives.

Unfortunately, women were often much more restricted in their movements than men. We do, however, have numerous accounts of travelling women from the Muslim world as well. They extend from the elite royal journeys of such women as Mughal Princess Gulbadan, who wrote a detailed account of her Hajj, to Awadh's Queen Mother Malika Keshwar, who, for the sake of petitioning Queen Victoria, travelled from Lucknow to London, passing away in Paris where her grave can still be found today. But there are also the numerous accounts of humble female travelling ascetics, such as the sufi mystic Fatima Sam who journeyed from Syria to Delhi. In the late nineteenth and early twentieth century, European women who had converted to Islam joined these female Muslim travellers. We may here mention Isabelle Eberhardt, a Swiss-born woman of German, Russian and Armenian heritage, who crossed the Sahara Desert multiple times and joined the Qadiri sufi order and Lady Evelyn Zainab Cobbold, a British aristocrat who performed the Hajj, all on her own in a motor car and wrote a best-selling book about it in 1934. For many of these women their journeys were also an exploration of gender and womanhood, a way to reflect upon the constraints that their native societies had put on them and, equally, to compare them to the constraints of other societies.

In many ways I see my own journey as undertaken within the tradition of these travellers, both the more recent European female Muslim travellers and the classical *rihla 'ilmiyya*. Long before I actually began this physical journey, however, the roots for my quest to understand myself, my faith and my gender had already been planted in the small rural German town that I grew up in.

Imagine a little queer kid of maybe six years old. At that age it is hard to tell whether the child is a girl or a boy, but they are a beautiful child, nevertheless. Their mother always wants them to cut their hair short, but it is a struggle each time; the child prefers to keep it long. Imagine a scene in which the child, covered in multiple transparent veils, has a scarf bound around their hips. Music plays in the background. It is a birthday party and other children are standing around, watching the queer child. The voice of the Egyptian-Lebanese singer Farid El-Atrache plays in the background. A bouncing Arabic tune. The child is waving his or her hips and arms, dancing. Belly-dancing, as the other children call it, who are half admiring it, half laughing about it. This is how it started...

It has nowadays become uncommon and despised amongst trans people to talk about what is called one's 'dead name'. That is, the name that was given before gender reassignment, corresponding to the gender assigned at birth. I have to admit that I have a very uneasy relationship with my 'dead name' as well. It is necessary that I mention it here though, because it played such an important role in my sense of cultural identity and how I became the person that I am now. I was born in a rural German community in 1980 and I was named Nikos Jagiella. Back then, it was a slightly confusing name for the almost monolithically white community I grew up in. It was a name that was definitely not considered German but whose origins people were unsure of. A first name very immediately identifiable as Greek by most who heard it, and a Polish family name that, nevertheless, still seems ambiguous to a lot of people. Only people well-versed in Eastern European history can usually identify its origins correctly. In any case, my dead name was a name that, right from the beginning, marked me as very different from the community that I grew up in.

Another thing which marked me as different was my gender expression. I had been assigned male at birth and was brought up as a boy, but I was never very happy with that label. I cannot say for sure whether I always identified clearly as a girl, but I did identify with the girls and women around me and was attracted to doing things that were labelled 'feminine' by society. I preferred to play with dolls, for example, and loved to try out my mom's make-up. However, the social expectations surrounding my body were in conflict with how I felt about myself. My parents and grandparents worried about my unusual preferences sometimes, but they loved me, wanted me to be happy, and at that stage they tried not to be too perturbed with my choice of games and toys. I was lucky in that respect.

Nevertheless, conflicts surrounding my queer behaviour were ever present. Neighbours, the kindergarten staff and, later, primary school teachers often commented negatively on my mannerisms and behaviour. Other boys treated me quite badly at times, and other girls sometimes did not want to play with me because, to them, I was a boy. I remember on several occasions I begged my mom, tears running down my face, not to send me to school or kindergarten because my experiences there were sometimes traumatic. It was not only that the other children could be quite cruel but the teachers and parents as well. I cried a lot as a child and felt horribly lonely at times.

My story is a rather familiar one in that regard, close to the script. I would caution people not to generalise my experience; playing with dolls does not make one a girl, neither does experimenting with make-up. But in my case, and in the case of many others, these things are often seen as cultural markers of femininity. And they were part of the puzzle that led me to explore my own gender identity.

Very early on I sought refuge from the burden of the real world in make-believe, daydreaming and fantasy, especially in books. As soon as I started to learn to read, I developed a passion for exploring the roots of human civilisation. I therefore became determined very early on in life to become either an archaeologist or an anthropologist when I grew up. My first great love in that regard was ancient Egypt, and I developed a fascination for the strong queens of that realm, in particular women like Cleopatra or Hatshepsut. My passion for everything Egyptian was soon to be followed by an interest in ancient India and China. It is quite an odd thing to say about a primary school child but, along with my favourite dolls, some of the best presents my parents ever gave me as a little child were visits to museum exhibitions, or gifts of exhibition catalogues. The treasure of the diversity that ancient cultures seemed to offer made me happy and helped me forget the less happy parts of my life.

Movies were another important opportunity to escape, and offered a source of role models for me as well. Like many queer kids of my generation, I harboured an early fascination with the tragic but strong feminine women on the silver screen. I felt empowered by these inspiring actresses and the dramatic characters they portrayed. Identifying with them helped me to face the bullying and pain that I was experiencing. Two of the first women I learned to love from an early age were Hollywood stars Bette Davis and Vivien Leigh. A few years later I discovered the dancing divas of classic Egyptian movies: Samia Gamal, Tahiya Carioca and Naima Akef. Finally, I fell in love with the alluring stars of early Indian cinema: Nargis, Madhubala, Waheeda Rehman and, more than anybody else, Meena Kumari. These early screen divas were headstrong, resilient, courageous and intelligent, while at the same time very much in touch with a femininity and sensuality that they consciously used for their own empowerment. Indeed, Islamic storytelling has a long tradition of resilient female characters that show intelligence and elegance in equal measure, starting with the famous Scheherazade of *Arabian Nights* and Dil-Aram of the *Hamzanama* epic. The female characters of classic Western literature and film, in comparison, seemed to me rather flat and less well equipped to make intelligent decisions.

My choice of Arab and Indian divas as role models was not a very natural one given that I had no Arab or South Asian ancestry. It was certainly a choice that was out of place in the small, very rural German town I grew up in. The town had, at that time, an almost uniformly white German population and most people living there were, to some degree or other, related to each other; their families had likely lived in the town, or at least the nearby region, for the last few centuries. My parents belonged to some of the first people who had moved there from elsewhere. Both of my parents had grown up in the Ruhrgebiet, an industrial, urban region that since the late nineteenth century had been marked by repeated waves of working-class immigration.

A TRANSNATIONAL JOURNEY

The Jagiellas, my father's side of the family, had originally migrated to the Ruhrgebiet from a small village in the vicinity of Gniezno in Central Poland. Family lore says that they were not natives of that region but had migrated to Central Poland from further East. It has been claimed that the Jagiellas had some connection to the Lithuanian Jagiellonian dynasty that once ruled the Kingdom of Poland. This seems a little spurious, however, as names derived from the dynasty and its founder, King Jagiello, are not rare in Poland at all. Another legend, which had a far more pervasive influence on me in early childhood, was that the Jagiellas may have had distant Tatar Muslim ancestry. There had indeed been a minority of Tatar Muslims in Poland since the days of King Jagiello (around 1400) and while there are still a few Tatar Muslim villages in the East of Poland nowadays, many had, over the centuries, adopted the Catholic faith and become 'proper Poles'. Despite Poland being today a largely mono-ethnic and mono-religious country, its history has been far more diverse. Muslim Tatars once played a prominent role in Poland; and Islam, as Polish-American writer Jacob Mikanowski once put it, runs 'like a silver thread' throughout Polish and Eastern European cultural history. Whether of actual Tatar descent or not, I identify with the diversity of Polish history, the memory of which is increasingly repressed in a nationalist Poland today.

In my recent family history, there was a more tangible manifestation of the entangled histories of Eastern and Eastern Central Europe. My paternal grandmother's father had, at the time of World War I and in the years immediately after, lived and worked in late-Ottoman Istanbul. He was of mixed German, Polish and Lithuanian origin and came from a part of Europe that was once ruled by the Polish crown, had been under Prussian occupation at the time of his birth, and then for a decade during his lifetime was split between Germany and independent Lithuania (with his family and relatives equally split). Nowadays it belongs to the

Russian Kaliningrad Oblast. Opportunities for work were very bleak in that impoverished and marginalised border region, which made him seek his fortunes elsewhere.

He would later bring his family to the Ruhrgebiet but Ottoman Istanbul was his first destination and he remained there for quite a while. He may have also had an interest in Islam: my grandmother once remarked that her father was not very fond of the Church and apparently considered Islam the far more rational religion. In my grandparents' home there was a Turkish carpet that he had once brought over from there. There were colourised postcards of the sights of Istanbul, with printed Ottoman script, and a portrait of my great-grandfather in the dress of a late Ottoman gentleman, wearing a tarbush and smoking a hookah. These remnants of life in the Ottoman Empire always drew my special attention and offered another opportunity to escape from the world around me.

Despite these remnants of a more culturally complex past, however, my father's family was one that had actively sought assimilation into German mainstream society right after immigrating to the Ruhrgebiet. My grandfather had even changed his name Kazimierz (which had already been Germanised into Kasimir) to Karl and had converted from Catholicism to Protestantism. Nobody wanted to be Polish in post-World War II and Cold War Germany, as being Slavic was considered the next best thing to being brown in the charged nationalist atmosphere of the country. The German majority identified Poles with theft, dirt and disorder, and racist jokes about Poles were as common as racist jokes about Turks and Jews.

Admitting a history of migration was a problematic thing in Germany in any case. The idea of a 'real German' is a very strongly racialised one and is not really comparable to nationalist sentiments in other European countries. It is virtually impossible to ever 'become' German, no matter how long you have stayed in the country. In fact, it often takes several generations until a family can be accepted as part of German society. Even now, many decades on, children whose families migrated to Germany from Turkey four generations ago are identified as 'Turkish'—not even 'German Turkish'—and 'Ausländer' (foreigners) by German mainstream society. In that way, total assimilation was, and in many ways still is, the only way to be fully accepted as German. For Polish immigrants that path was always more accessible than to other immigrants since most were not constrained by racial markers that would eternally mark them as 'other'.

As such, I grew up with knowledge of my Polish origins but only very few immediate connections to Polish language or culture. The general message was, 'We are in Germany now, let's try to be as German as possible.' This bothered me. Why was it such a problem to speak about our origins? Why was it so important to belong to this particular people but not that particular people? The most important question for me was: why could one not be several things at the same time? My mother's family was in many ways very different from my father's family, though its history raised similar questions about singular and multiple belongings for me. While my paternal grandfather had been a coal miner, my mother's father was a theologian. A gentle man who had been born into a very humble rural German family, he managed to study Protestant theology at university and become an ordained Lutheran clergyman. He loved classical European education and next to the Bible he regularly read Roman and Greek mythology. He also spoke Italian fluently and had spent several years of his life in Italy. During the Nazi period he had been an active member of the 'Bekennende Kirche', the Protestant church resistance. It was in those circles that he had met my grandmother, who came from a very different background.

My maternal grandmother descended on one side from an aristocratic family that had for centuries settled on both sides of the Polish-German border, and on the other side had roots in late-imperial Russian St. Petersburg. My grandmother placed high value on this noble and cosmopolitan descent and, since she found in me an eager ear interested in family history, she impressed that value on me early on. My grandfather and grandmother lived in a small apartment in one of the cities of the Ruhrgebiet. Almost all of my grandmother's siblings led humble existences, very different from the grand manors and huge villas their family had once possessed in Poland and Russia. But even in that world there existed vestiges of the imperial past which drew my attention. Heavy St. Petersburg silver and Orthodox Christian icons. The old Uzbek ceramics which one of my grandmother's sisters had added to the dowry of my mother when she married my father.

The upper-class cosmopolitan history of my maternal grandmother's family contained a few connections to the Islamic world as well. My grandmother's ancestry could, through Polish and Russian nobility, be traced back to a medieval Armenian family which had once occupied important positions both in the Byzantine Empire and under Arab Muslim rule. In much more recent times, my grandmother's family had, after fleeing the October Revolution, been stationed for many years in Istanbul, an important hub for exiled Russians at that time. An uncle of my grandmother's had also settled down and married in Istanbul in the 1920s. When I visit Istanbul, I still sometimes go to the cemetery in Feriköy to say a prayer at his withered grave.

My grandmother had also told me of our distant relatives in India. In the nineteenth century, my grandmother's family had been closely associated with the Gossner mission, a mission that had once been active in St. Petersburg, which tried to unite Orthodox, Catholic and Protestant Christians, but which had later focused its attention on Christianising the indigenous Oraon people of Indian Chotanagpur (now Jharkhand). A cousin of her St. Petersburg family had married a very prominent German Gossner missionary and had moved to present-day Jharkhand with him. That branch of the family was to stay in India for five generations. It was many decades later that I was able to reconnect with a cousin from that line. I met Mary Girard, who, like the late Indian actor Tom Alter, was an alumni of Mussoorie's Woodstock School in the foothills of the Himalayas, while we were both in Delhi in 2017. I was surprised to click so easily with her and find someone not only related in blood, but in spirit. In her book, *Among the Original Dwellers* (2019), Mary tells the story of her ancestors, the nineteenth-century Gossner mission to the Oraon and how a missionary venture ended up playing 'a significant role in helping the Adivasi retain their culture and fight for their liberation'.

I am, of course, constructing a far too convenient narrative of a cosmopolitan family of many roots here. There are, equally, several aspects of my family history which disrupt that narrative. My grandmother has an uncle who was a supporter of the Nazi party. In fact, her own parents once supported the Nazis in the hope that Hitler would restore the old imperial order of the world that existed before World War I and the October Revolution. I should add that I had a special interest in listening to stories of origins and seeking out remnants of a cosmopolitan past in my surroundings. Perhaps this was because, as far as my gender was concerned, I had already experienced a strong sense of alienation from the society I grew up in. Not everybody in my family attributed the same weight of belonging and identity to these things. My father in particular always insisted that all that mattered to his sense of cultural identity was being in Germany now. Most of my relatives have become quite comfortable with a German middle-class identity.

The most pervasive influence on my sense of belonging came from my immediate family surroundings, in particular, from my parents' own cultural infatuation with Greece. Neither were particularly rooted in Polish or Russian identity but they developed a passion for Greek culture as a young couple, getting engaged on the island of Rhodes and spending their honeymoon in Greek Makedonia. When I, their first child, was born they decided to baptise me with a very Greek male name: Nikos. Later, when my younger brother was born, he was baptised with another Greek name, Janis (pronounced Yannis). On numerous occasions throughout my childhood I have been misidentified by others as Greek. Greek culture was indeed very familiar to me, since my parents' love for it led to many long summer stays in the country. I grew up with Greek music and Greek food. But we were not Greek.

As already indicated, many Germans are very particular when it comes to their idea of who a 'real' German is, and German racism often manifests itself in a fixation upon a person's name. In the small town that I grew up in, my Greek first name and ambiguous-sounding Polish surname marked me as 'other'. For my whole life I have been confronted with the question that immigrant children always get: 'But where are you really from?' This question always carried the implication that I was not 'really German'. At some point, I started to willingly embrace this 'otherness'.

While I cannot compare my story to those of countless others who have had to battle more violent and explicit racism in German society, paired with the bullying and ostracism I experienced because of my gender identity, my name and family background gave me an eternal sense of 'never belonging'. It taught me very early on in life that I had to create a niche of my own in this world, both beyond a narrowly constructed gender binary and beyond equally narrowly constructed religious, cultural and national identities. Early on in life I developed a healthy scepticism of all essentialised identities. What is a 'real German', a 'real Pole', a 'real Russian' or a 'real Greek'? What is a 'real boy' or a 'real girl'? And what holds the key to the truth about ourselves?

Is it the stories that we tell about ourselves? Or the stories that others tell about us? Both? Or neither?

Fed by multiple, multicoloured streams, my identity formed, not firmly rooted in one nor the other, but very much defined by a feeling of distance and lack of belonging to the German small-town culture surrounding me. That is what gave birth to the little queer belly-dancing kid at the birthday party.

This constant sense of 'not belonging' eventually led me on a spiritual journey as well. The stories of possible Tatar ancestors, my great-grandfather's Ottoman pictures, an early familiarity with Eastern Mediterranean music, dance, food and culture and a passion for Egypt and India led me to an interest in Islam. I was very interested in religious questions as a child. Thanks to my maternal grandfather, the aforementioned Lutheran clergyman, religion had always been a topic of conversation at home, even though my parents were not very religious at all. My interest in ancient cultures had exposed me to a wealth of different religious ideas and at an early age I started to wonder what the final truth was behind all of this. More than anything, I also wanted to find out what the truth was behind my life. Why are some human beings born different? And why does that cause them so much suffering? Was there a meaning behind all of this?

Somehow, Islam appeared to be the best answer to my questions. I was attracted to it aesthetically: the amazing love of beauty expressed in its art, the majestic emptiness of its mosques, the ethereal charm of the call to prayer. But I was also very attracted by its theology: Islam gave me a philosophy with which to understand my reality. The idea that there is a Divine Unity at the centre of existence, one that nevertheless manifests in the multiplicity of human expression, appealed to me and gave me a framework to understand my experiences of non-belonging and otherness. As a sceptic of all essentialised identity I could now with conviction say: The only thing that is actually real (al-

Haqq) is God (Allah). There is nothing essential but Him. Everything else is just the endless diversity that His boundless unity expresses itself in.

I had started to incorporate Islam into my life long before I made the official decision to change my religion. My parents still possess an old VHS recording from the 1980s on which one can see me perform the moves of Muslim ritual prayer in an old, ruined Ottoman mosque in Greece. I must have been about eight years old at that time and I had already taught myself how to pray Islamically. When I was twelve years old, at a local German Turkish mosque, I contemplated officially becoming Muslim. Two years later, at the age of fourteen, I started to regularly visit that same mosque.

At that time, my body was changing rapidly. Puberty had arrived: the age when hormones flood your body and change its appearance forever, the time when you become aware of your own sexuality. Up until that age, my genderqueer behaviour had been of an innocent nature. Puberty suddenly changed everything. I discovered that in addition to my existing identification with all things feminine, I was also developing romantic and sexual interests in men. This new interest felt as natural to me as my childhood interests; there was nothing strange about it as such. But society, I discovered again, saw things differently.

I watched jealously when some of my female friends started to flirt with boys who certainly appreciated their attention. Boys categorically did not appreciate my attention. For some time I saw myself as gay and I wondered if I could find love and fulfilment in the gay community. But after a while it became clear to me that that was not what I wanted. I never wanted to be attractive to a man 'as a man'. I experienced myself as a young woman, with the feelings and desires of a young woman, albeit with a body that felt increasingly at odds with my inner feelings and self-perception. I felt as if I was in a prison. A prison whose walls were getting narrower and narrower every day, threatening to crush me.

The situation became even more complicated because of my involvement in the local mosque. There I entered a world that was strictly defined by gender segregation. I was perceived as a boy and had to conform to the standards created for boys. I was not allowed to pray with women and girls to whom I felt much closer emotionally and in whose company I felt much more safe. I started to have crushes on the boys at the mosque and was always afraid that they would eventually find out and chastise me for it. Eventually I created a double life. At school I discussed make-up and the latest boy bands with my female friends, while at the mosque I tried to be a 'good Muslim boy'. Both were part of my life and both were important to me but I couldn't see any way of reconciling the two.

In numerous Friday sermons, I learned that homosexual and cross-gendered feelings were supposedly sinful. From time to time I tried to repent, to 'pray the gay away', as they say. I threw away all of the make-up I had started to use at school with non-Muslim friends and devoted myself to strenuous religious exercises that were supposed to make me 'normal'. Alas, they never fulfilled this promise. What they did do, however, was momentarily suppress my natural traits and feelings, which only returned with a vengeance after a short while, creating a self-destructive backlash of uncontrollable negative emotions and unbalanced sexual desires.

My parents became concerned about me and my 'eccentric behaviour'. There was a moment when I confessed to them that 'I might be gay or something similar'. Their reply was that they would always love me but would nevertheless prefer me to keep my 'sexual orientation' (or whatever it was) to myself. We did live in a small rural town, after all, and my oddities did not help much with any desire to assimilate. They had already become increasingly unhappy with me when I declared my official conversion to Islam. With all of my choices I seemed to mock their own desires for normality and belonging.

Thus my teenage years were spent fighting on different fronts simultaneously. There was the discovery of my own identity and sexuality in the midst of the sometimes cruel environment of hormone-intoxicated teenagers. There was my constant struggle at the mosque and with my Muslim friends to present myself as a 'normal boy' devoted to Muslim orthodoxy. And then there were regular skirmishes with my family. Sometimes I could hardly bear all the pressure. Dealing with constant criticism from several sections of the outside world was one thing. Even worse was the fact that I internalised what others told me. Even though I knew with all my heart that there was nothing wrong with me and that I just felt the way that was most natural to me, I developed strong feelings of guilt and self-loathing. A clinical depression set in that has accompanied me ever since. When insults such as 'fag' or 'sissy' (or the German equivalents) were thrown at me, I always put all of the blame on myself. I eventually became highly suicidal. I probably would not have survived at that point without my strong faith in God and the support of some very good friends at school.

When I was nineteen and about to finish my school education, I realised that I had to change my life if I were to survive. If I did not make a clear decision to stand up for who I was and how I wanted to live, I would have no future whatsoever. This became evident when I was faced with insistent demands for gender conformity from the Muslim side of my life; *imams* and friends constantly advised me to get married—to a girl—as soon as possible. I also realised that I would be leaving my parents and hometown very soon to start higher education somewhere else. After yet another dramatic attempt to change myself and become 'normal', which, again, only ended in strange sexual escapades and suicidal thoughts, I decided that I had to start life as a woman. I knew that this was the only way for me to feel natural and socially adjusted.

At that time, I had already started to network online with people all over the world who had started to develop a more positive approach towards the place of LGBTQI people in Islam. Queer Muslims had started organising in the UK, South Africa, Canada and the US, the vast majority of them from South Asian family backgrounds. I also started to connect with people who were not part of the queer Muslim community but who, nevertheless, had started to think about Islam in innovative ways. I had had many years of intense discussions about the message of the Quran with the Malaysian-British Quranic journalist and thinker Farouk A. Peru, who would later introduce me to the London-based Muslim Institute.

My anthropological interests also encouraged me to explore transgender identities in several Muslim contexts. This led me to a few acquaintances who would prove crucial in my later development: I had started to communicate with a few Pakistani LGBT activists who later founded a short-lived online zine called *Humjinsparast* and had started to explore topics such as homosexuality and gender diversity from a decolonising perspective. Through them, I got to know the late Pakistani-German filmmaker Khalid Gill and his German-Polish wife Uxi who were working on a documentary on *khwajasaras* in Lahore. I eventually met American trans activist Anne Ogborn, who had become an initiated member of a *hijra gharana* in Delhi. Khalid Gill would later introduce me to the world of Pakistani *khwajasaras* in 2007. But long before that, it was Anne Ogborn who invited me to join her on a trip to her *dera* in Delhi in 2000.

My decision to transition had by then become firm but I knew that I wanted to make the first proper step towards that crucial change in India. It has now been more than twenty years since I stepped off the plane in Mumbai, where Annie awaited me. We headed towards the holy city of Ajmer Shareef in Rajasthan to meet the *hijras* from her *dera* there. I spent the first day of my life as a 'recognisable' woman, among the *hijras*, there at the *urs*, the annual festival that commemorates the death of the Muslim saint Khwaja Ghareeb Nawaz, may his secret be sanctified. I prayed at the shrine of the saint that God would open up all paths for me on this new journey. And He did. After that first trip with Annie, there followed many others on my own, learning about several *hijra* communities in India. I have, all in all, spent more than a year living in *deras* in India. I later spent time with the *khwajasara* community of Pakistan, to whom I feel especially close and indebted now. For two decades now, I have been walking on a path with the South Asian *hijra* and *khwajasara* communities, on which they have been my constant companion and have taught me a lot.

It is important to acknowledge the huge changes that our world has gone through in the course of that period, affecting many LGBT and queer issues. When I was born, male homosexuality was still criminalised in parts of the UK and it was not fully decriminalised in Germany until I was a young teenager. Many years on, both countries have introduced civil partnerships for homosexual couples and finally legalised marriage between same-sex couples, something which seemed entirely impossible when I was young. Forced surgery on intersex children, a form of genital mutilation, was very common in both countries for the larger part of my life. It still remains common today, but medical and legal attitudes towards it have changed for the better. Only since 2005 have transgender people been allowed to legally change their gender in the UK. In Germany, a very antiquated law regulating gender-reassignment has existed since 1980; it only underwent reform in 2011 based on more recent evaluations and medical knowledge.

On the level of representation, when I was young and in search of myself, there was not much talk about transgender issues in the West at all. The public visibility of transgender people was largely restricted to television freak shows and entertainment. When I visited India and encountered the *hijra* community in Delhi for the first time, I quickly became part of a very different world. While I was aware of issues of discrimination and marginalisation in Indian society, in comparison to us transgender women in Europe, my sisters in South Asia seemed much more aware of having a recognised place in society. Both in India and Pakistan, I witnessed the natural everyday visibility of the third gender in society, and despite the fact that strong prejudices existed in mainstream society against *hijras* and *khwajasaras*, their presence was treated as a far more normal part of life than in the West. At that time both Pakistan and India had looked to me much better-equipped for progress in transgender rights than any Western country.

A lot of positive change did indeed happen in South Asia in the years following my first visits. The pre-existing strong visibility of the third gender in Pakistan transformed into an increasingly prominent transgender activism with more and more activists visible in documentary films, movies and TV debates, and entering spaces such as politics, arts, acting or modelling. An official 'third gender' status was introduced in Pakistan in 2009, in India in 2011 and in Bangladesh in 2013. Anti-discrimination laws protecting the rights of *khwajasaras* and other transgender people were introduced in Pakistan in 2018. Unfortunately, South Asian countries do often still lag behind when it comes to the implementation of these laws. Furthermore, *hijra*, *khwajasara* and transgender communities still suffer immensely from a lack of education and financial resources and from discrimination in traditional workspaces.

Meanwhile, homosexuality has very much become a global battleground. Even though all LGBTQI rights in Western countries are relatively young and still highly contested, the West has now somehow come to imagine itself as a beacon of light for LGBTQI people, often positioning itself in positive contrast to other non-Western, particularly Muslim, countries. Being LGBTQI is now officially recognised as a legitimate reason to seek asylum in Western countries for people fleeing from countries where homosexuality is criminalised. At the same time, the hurdles that are set for people seeking asylum to jump over are very high and the process of seeking asylum is often extremely traumatic.

Just as Western countries have begun to portray themselves as defenders of LGBTQI people, other countries have, conversely, sought to portray themselves as vanguards of traditional values. Several Muslim majority nations are amongst these 'vanguards', as well as countries like Russia and Christian majority regions of countries such as Nigeria and Uganda. These two developments are not unrelated. A backlash of alleged (but often entirely imagined) 'traditional values' has also begun to threaten the safety of LGBTQI people in Western countries again. In the US, the Trump administration has wound back the clock on many achievements made in the past, banning transgender people from serving in the military and removing legal protections for those discriminated against in the workplace because of their gender identity. In Germany, a new popular right-wing party, the AfD, wants to curb LGBT rights, and in the UK a movement of trans-exclusionary radical feminists (TERFs) has gained currency even in purportedly liberal circles, gaining fresh wind thanks to the dialogue surrounding public interventions by famous writers such as J.K. Rowling.

2

THE UNBEARABLE WHITENESS OF BEING

WHEN A GROUP OF *hijras* out on *badhai* pass through the streets, they always attract a considerable amount of attention, for better or for worse. Even more eyes are drawn to that group when it includes a white '*hijra*'. Whenever I accompanied the girls on *badhai*, it tended to create a particular spectacle. People didn't quite know what to think of me. Sometimes they thought I was a journalist or researcher from the West. When they heard me speak Urdu, they were especially confused. My Urdu is far from perfect—I make a lot of mistakes—but I have been told that I speak it to quite a decent standard. My German accent, however, is not something that people in India and Pakistan are very used to; most white people speaking Hindi or Urdu they encounter or see on television have an English or North American accent. Once a lady blurted out, pointing at me: '*Vo Afghanistan se aayi hai?*' Did she come from Afghanistan?

At that time in Delhi, those with fair hair and fair skin who could speak a decent amount of Hindi/Urdu were often identified as Afghan. Despite the sad fact that Hindu nationalists in India often denounce Afghans as 'foreign invaders', Afghanistan has a long, shared history with Delhi. Both belonged to the same empire in antique Buddhist times, as well as under several Muslim ruling houses, and Delhi has also been ruled by Afghan dynasties. In the Mughal era, waves of immigrants from Afghanistan arrived in Delhi, with Hindu traders from today's Northern India and Pakistan settling in Afghanistan.[1] To separate the history of Afghanistan from the history of Delhi is, therefore, impossible. In the quarters that we visited during our *badhai* trips in the early 2000s, there lived a good number of Hindu and Sikh families who had originally come from Afghanistan in the 1980s, sometimes even earlier. They were commonly called *kabuli*. More recent Muslim refugees from Afghanistan had also arrived in the city.

There were a couple of *hijras* of Afghan origin in our *gharana*, just as there had also been a few *hijras* of Nepali and Bangladeshi origin. These *hijras* from different parts of South Asia were never treated as foreigners in the community. Many, though certainly not all, of these Hindus, Sikhs and Muslims of Afghan origin looked as fair as some white Europeans. Looking more closely at me, the woman in question would probably not have confused me with an Afghan. But it was, presumably, the ludicrousness of the idea of a European *hijra* on *badhai* that made her say what she did.

In my early twenties, having just escaped the world of a small German town and a small German Turkish mosque, I was, somewhat naively, elated when I heard the woman's question. I wanted to be taken seriously as part of the fabric of the *hijra* community of Delhi; to not be immediately recognised as a European made me feel I truly belonged there. I did not want to be seen as a European visitor 'finding herself' in India. I saw myself as belonging to this *hijra gharana* in a way that a 'real European' usually could not.

There were a couple of other experiences which confirmed this impression of mine. On my very first trip to Delhi, when I accompanied Anne Ogborn, the girls often remarked to me that I seemed to tolerate Indian food—real Indian food, not the type cooked in fancy hotels—much better than Anne did. Being Muslim also immediately raised the esteem that the older gurus of the *dera* had for me. A few years later, when I spent time on my own in another *dera*, I was often complimented on how comfortable I seemed in India and how well I fitted into the community. Many of my sisters remarked that they couldn't believe that I was a Westerner.

THE UNBEARABLE WHITENESS OF BEING

I remember one time when we were out on *badhai* and having some food at a roadside stall. My sister Sunita had been observing me: how I behaved; how I walked; how I brushed my hair; how I ate my food. After observing me for a while, she suddenly said, *'Tum aadhaa Hindustani ho.'* You are half-Indian. From then on, other sisters repeated that phrase whenever they noticed me do or say something they found commendable. 'You are half-Indian.' Sometimes people called me Helen, referring to the famed Anglo-Indian Bollywood star of the same name, or compared me to the actress Priya Rajvansh, who had an English mother and had grown up in the UK. The old grandmother guru at our *dera* always praised me for regularly praying my ritual prayers, using the appropriate Muslim phrases in my everyday dealings and not secretly drinking alcohol and partying like some of her other *chelas*. *'Tum meri asli musalmaan bacchi ho.'* You are my real Muslim child.

These words made a huge impression on me. Even more so since I still carried an acutely painful feeling of never belonging in my heart. I felt that, maybe here, I could finally belong.

That sense of belonging, however, was a fragile one, something that became clear to me as soon as I experienced conflict with other members of the community. Just as in any other family or community, internal conflicts exist in every *dera* and *gharana*. It is expected from all *chelas* that, in order not to harm the integrity of the community, these conflicts should be managed according to the traditional hierarchies, with all disputes and punishments being settled by the jurisdiction of the gurus. As someone who grew up very differently from my other sisters, I did not easily accept these hierarchies as a given. I knew that my sisters respected these hierarchies; I too romanticised them for a long time. But the truth is, I valued my own sense of individual freedom over being indebted to the authority structures of a collective.

When I disagreed with something I saw in the community, I would do so loudly and visibly and was hence marked as very bad-mannered. Once, at dinner, I noticed an elder sister sitting across from me badmouthing me in front of one of the gurus. I made a rude gesture in the sister's direction, but unfortunately the guru thought that it was directed at her. I was told to go to my room and hide for the next few days, a rather mild punishment compared to other traditional punishments common in the community. My individual share in the earnings of the *badhai* was cut. From then on, the tone towards me changed considerably. I was not 'half-Indian' anymore. Instead I was referred to as '*Vo angrezan*'. That Englishwoman. I was hurt. Being stripped of my new sense of belonging so suddenly hurt more than anything else. But I had clearly brought it upon myself, by behaving like an *angrezan*.

These were familiar dynamics across the twenty years of my history with the *hijra* and *khwajasara* community. Every now and then people confirmed to me that I did not seem like a white European, making me feel validated and providing me with a sense of belonging. I remember one time, during an international film festival attended by many other Westerners, the partner of a Pakistani *khwajasara* friend remarked that talking to me never felt like talking to a 'Westerner'. I often received the same sense of validation outside of the *hijra* and *khwajasara* communities. The mother of a good friend living in Old Delhi always remarked that I seemed Indian to her. My life partner of the past few years is Pakistani and the topic comes up frequently when speaking with friends and acquaintances. Once a friend of my partner asked me, 'So, are both of your parents from Pakistan, or only one?' We could only laugh.

My time in India has become an integral part of my own self-conception, built into my very being. It is not just that I speak Urdu and have acquired a considerable amount of knowledge about South Asian cultures; the fact that I spent a very formative period of my early twenties in India, transitioning there, has influenced me strongly. I remember that around 2010, I had gone through a period of particularly strong conflict with members of the *hijra* community in India. There was so much grief on both sides that for a while I questioned whether I ever wanted to return to South Asia. It was only very shortly after this that I was invited to India for another event. As soon as I stepped off the plane, I felt an overwhelming sense of home—something I feel nowhere else in the world but India and Pakistan.

Whenever conflicts arise between myself and members of the community in India and Pakistan, I feel my sense of belonging diminish. Many of these conflicts have centred around very real issues of privilege—privilege which I have and which many of my Indian and Pakistani sisters do not share. The most obvious of these privileges is that there is no real necessity for me to accept traditional rules and hierarchies because I can just leave and fly back to my country of origin as soon as I want to. None of my South Asian sisters has that luxury. Another point of contention has always been money. *Hijras* and *khwajasaras* do not have the benefit of relying on social structures such as birth families, neighbourhood networks or village *panchayats* (councils). As part of a marginalised minority, many do not have access to good education or financial and employment security. When I fly in from the other side of the planet, it always highlights the fact that I lead a far more financially secure life.

When I visited Pakistan in 2017, I was only able to do so because I was invited to special occasions such as the Aks International Minorities Film Festival, and graciously funded by international donors. I was unemployed at that time and did not receive benefits. Unfortunately, on arrival in Pakistan, a considerable amount of money was stolen from my person and so I ended up completely broke. I have often been in similar situations when visiting Pakistan and, in such situations, I have counted on the hospitality of my Pakistani sisters. Yet, even when facing my own financial difficulties, my situation was still far more financially stable than any of my Pakistani sisters' was. I could always rely on good health insurance in Germany. If need be, I could always rely on my family to get by. Even though I was unemployed, I was never at risk of dying of hunger on the streets, something that can be a very real danger for many of my sisters in India and Pakistan, especially when involved in conflicts with their *dera* or *gharana*, which would usually provide for them. By relying on their hospitality in these situations, I was actually overextending my claim on their resources, no matter how harsh my own situation.

Validations in the form of 'You are half-Indian' or 'You don't seem Western at all' made me forget the differences that existed between me and my Pakistani and Indian sisters. That naturally made me feel good because privileged people never like to be reminded of their privilege. Privilege always comes with feelings of guilt, especially if it is privilege that we were born with and that we did not achieve through work. This poses a specific internal problem for those of us who feel underprivileged in many other ways. What has been labelled an 'Oppression Olympics' has become a hallmark of much of the social and political discourse of our day and age. In my own case, I wanted people to acknowledge how difficult my own struggles as a transgender woman were. However, focusing on our own experiences of discrimination and marginalisation can sometimes prevent us from addressing our privileges, leading us to place the guilt on others.

These 'Oppression Olympics', together with a strong essentialisation of identity, have created a set of particularly strange dynamics that have led some people to try to cover up their own privileges in shocking ways. In 2015, Rachel Dolezal, a woman born to white parents, was exposed for posing as an African-

American woman and gaining both influence and benefits as a Black activist. Her case caused a scandal in the US and was widely discussed around the world. Since then, several other similar cases have been uncovered. In 2020, George Washington University professor and activist Jessica Krug admitted that she, a child of Jewish parents, had posed as a Black Latina woman for many years. Wisconsin University teacher CV Vitolo-Haddad has recently come out with a very similar story. In Germany, we have long known of a similar phenomenon—several stories have come to light of white Germans posing as Jewish grandchildren of Holocaust survivors.

It is not an easy thing to admit, but my own experiences lead me to understand the motivation of people like Rachel Dolezal. Her story is very different from mine, but I identify in it a similar deep feeling of 'not-belonging', caused by a complicated, sometimes traumatic, upbringing, combined with finding a sense of belonging within a culture she was not born into. I also recognise in her many of my own defensive feelings when confronted with my privileges. If life had developed a little differently in my case, I could have easily fallen into the same traps that she fell into. I could have answered, 'Yes, I am from Afghanistan' to the woman in Delhi. I could have constructed a story of somehow being of South Asian descent when people saw me like that. By doing so, I would undoubtedly have committed the same injustices and caused the same harm that Rachel Dolezal did. The thought terrifies me.

Another anecdote illustrates my point here. In 2019, I spoke about Muslim trans issues at an international art event in Hamburg. One of the artists present was the wonderful queer Pakistani Lebanese performer Zulfikar Ali Bhutto Jr, also known by his drag name Faluda Islam. Zulfikar and I were happy to find in each other someone with whom we could discuss experiences of being queer in Pakistan, as well as exchange a few words in

Urdu. My talk was well-received by an audience mostly consisting of queer artists from various Muslim contexts. During my talk an Egyptian activist and artist started tweeting some of the things that I had said, describing me as 'Pakistani trans activist Leyla Jagiella'. Her tweets must have led to some comments from people who knew me better, as after my talk, she approached me, asking me to confirm that I was indeed Pakistani. I was horrified. Was this the beginning of my Rachel Dolezal story? Would I be publicly denounced by online activists and exposed for cultural appropriation? Fortunately for me, this did not happen, though I remain aware of the possible implications of such an incident.

Even more than one of cultural appropriation, I am very conscious of the fact that my experiences could easily be read as some kind of *Eat, Pray, Love* story—the emblematic example of a white Western woman using the backdrop of a journey to India (and beyond) as an exotic canvas on which to paint her own story of self-discovery. Although staying in a *hijra dera*, sleeping on the floor with the other girls and going out every day on *badhai* is certainly a different experience to spending time at a yoga *ashram* in Rishikesh, I do recognise that I am still a European woman with white privilege who went to India to understand herself better.

It took me quite a while to admit this fact, however. The realisation that I had something called 'privilege' did not come easily to me. For the first twenty years of my life, I felt constantly marginalised. I have already written extensively about my constant feeling of 'not belonging', as a young genderqueer person; as the person with the strange name who was never viewed as 'properly German'; and as a Muslim in a society which, during the course of my life, has become increasingly more Islamophobic. For many years I have suffered from depression and anxiety, not experiencing myself as a functioning human being. From that point of view, I always considered it natural that I should understand myself as belonging to the 'oppressed of the world', or at least as an obvious ally. I was blind to the fact that there were many things which gave me an advantage: birth in the rich Global North; a secure and comfortable family home; access to a brilliant education; a German passport; and being a white European.

There was a time in my life when I would have said that I do not believe that race matters. And, in essence, I still believe that race is a social construct and that it should indeed not matter. But the fact is that several centuries of European colonialism and imperialism have imprinted racism on our world in such a way that its material effects cannot be ignored. This history has made race a matter of fact and that matter of fact is felt in particularly brutal ways by those considered inferior within this racial hierarchy. To those who benefit from racial privilege, this is often invisible. When told about the prevalence of racism in our societies, many white people react with disbelief and denial. Discourses around race in our societies are also often inextricably tied to discourses around gender and sexuality. More than once, when I have told acquaintances of the transphobic experiences that I am still regularly faced with in Germany or the UK, my acquaintances have asked of my assaulters: 'And were they "real Germans", or were they immigrants?' The narrative that homophobia and transphobia are imported into German society by intolerant conservative Muslims is pervasive. I have also been met with reactions of disbelief on some occasions when I have told heterosexual, cisgender acquaintances of these transphobic experiences: 'Really?'; 'Are you sure?'; 'You may have misunderstood the situation?'; 'But this is impossible! People act that way?' Like other structural privileges, cisgender privilege often manifests itself in expressions of scepticism and repudiation.

In *Why I am a Five Percenter* (2011), Michael Muhammad Knight describes his journey from being a young, white American boy growing up in an openly racist environment to converting to

Islam, seeking a *madrasa* education in South Asia and eventually engaging with the Islamicate Black nationalists, the Five Percenters. He points out something that I have also experienced: white converts often entertain the notion that having converted to Islam, they somehow also get rid of their whiteness. This notion is sometimes supported by some Muslims of colour who want to see their religious community as more morally advanced than racist societies in the West. The Prophet Muhammad, peace be upon him and his family, in his last sermon indeed emphasised that descent and race should not matter, that all Muslims are brothers and that it is only the degree of piety that should mark one Muslim as better than another. But this ideal has never become fully manifest in the Muslim world.

Only a few decades after the death of the Prophet, under the Umayyad dynasty, legal distinctions were made between those of Arab and those of non-Arab descent. In many Arab societies even today, being black is immediately associated with being of slave descent and people are treated accordingly. From a very different position, many white Muslim converts comment on experiencing ostracism and remark that they are not as socially integrated into Muslim communities as born Muslims are. They are, conversely, also admired, idealised and romanticised. Women who are white converts are often sought after as marriage partners. While white male converts can usually continue to walk through everyday society with the same white privilege that they possessed before their conversion, for a woman it is a bit different if she chooses to wear a hijab in public.

Muhammad Knight also states that it was to some extent his experiences in Pakistan which made him question the idea of the 'raceless convert', and when I read his observations on life as a white American in Pakistan, I found myself nodding in agreement. Unlike him, I had not spent time in a South Asian *madrasa*. But living in a *hijra dera* across from a *madrasa* offered me some very similar insights. It was only after living in India and Pakistan for a while that I fully understood the reality of my own white privilege. It has often been noted that the British colonial regime was one of the most severe and rigid when it came to constructing racial realities. The atrocities committed under Spanish, French, Portuguese and Dutch colonial regimes are plenty, but these empires still allowed far more flexibility in their racial hierarchies than the British did. Perhaps only the Germans were more extreme than the British in that respect.

In South Asia the colonial British regime consciously strengthened and cemented pre-existing hierarchies and social differences (between castes, ethnic groups and religious communities) and incorporated these into a nineteenth-century pseudo-scientific system that viewed Western and Northern Europeans, and the British in particular, as superior, the pinnacle of creation. This created a toxic ideology whose effects still persist in South Asia today. It has returned with a vengeance in the Aryan cult of Hindu nationalism in India, but realities of casteism and colourism are no less in Muslim majority Pakistan. In fact, one could say that this system generated the conditions for the creation of the independent states of India and Pakistan in 1947, which have ever since been locked in a cycle of war and conflict with each other. Equally, ethnic and racial discrimination with its roots in the colonial era was a major factor in the civil turmoil and political violence between East and West Pakistan in the 1960s, leading to Bangladesh's independence in 1971.

Moving as a white person in South Asia, one either has to be completely blind to the realities produced by this history or one will find them nearly everywhere. I may have felt hurt when, after some conflict, my sisters would call me '*angrezan*', but the truth is that I could at any moment in time become an 'Englishwoman' and be accepted accordingly. I could dress up a bit differently and walk without hindrances through the gates of the Imperial Hotel and have high tea there whenever I liked, something that my sisters in the *dera* were not able to do. Even when confronted with issues of transphobia or homophobia I could always sport my German passport and claim that my embassy would intervene if people mistreated me further. That trick always worked. I was always considered more beautiful than my sisters, even though many of them were far more glamorous than I was, simply because colonial hang-ups have created the idea that whiteness equates to beauty. I was also, in general, often treated with far more respect by mainstream society in India and Pakistan than many of my local sisters were. In South Asia, I could enjoy the benefits of white privilege while at the same time feel the comfort of a Muslim transgender community that I never felt in Europe.

I have already spoken a little about the history of Muslim travellers who explored the world. I should here also speak of the fact that there is a history of queer Westerners travelling to Muslim countries in order to experience a tolerance towards expressions of sexuality and gender not known at home. In the late nineteenth and early twentieth century in particular, homosexual and bisexual writers and artists like Oscar Wilde, William S. Burroughs, Paul Bowles, Allen Ginsberg, Tennessee Williams, Yves Saint Laurent and many more travelled to North Africa or even settled down there for a while. The sexual dealings of some of these artists were clearly of an abusive and questionable nature, since many of their interactions were with those who were highly dependent on their foreign friends and often underage. Celebrating their freedom from their own native constraints, the Europeans did not appreciate the constraints their lovers were in.

From the 1950s to the 1970s, a large number of Western transgender women also flocked to North Africa, at a time when Morocco was the world hub of gender reassignment surgery. There is a whole generation of famous European transgender women who underwent gender reassignment surgery in Casablanca where legal limitations on such surgeries did not exist and where prices were more affordable. It is true that at that time most Muslim societies were in general far more tolerant of sexual diversity than most Western societies and had a far more relaxed attitude to both homosexuality and expressions of transgender identity. However, it is also true that many of these Western travellers relied upon their privileged backgrounds to get themselves out of any trouble. North African cities like Alexandria, Tangier and Casablanca were vibrant cosmopolitan hubs in which being European was for a long time considered equivalent to being upper class.

On an individual level, I would hope that I am better than these earlier queer travellers searching for fulfilment in 'the Orient'. However, since the world is still largely organised according to the same colonial-era hierarchies, I have to accept that structurally I may not be. I have spent a considerable amount of time worrying about these issues and contemplating them. In the end, my answer is that we can only deal with these issues if we accept the given realities of our positions. I am a privileged white European. I am also the product of my family's history of migration. I am a Muslim woman. I am a transgender woman. And I am a person who has been influenced by a formative time spent in South Asia during my adolescent years. I cannot become a different person. Even though all of these different parts of my identity feel very disparate and contradictory at times, and even though I still battle that haunting feeling of 'not belonging', all of this is part of me, my pain and struggle with it as much as all my privilege and arrogance.

I have often felt that if there truly is a space that I can belong to then it will always be the space 'in-between'. That is as much true for my experience of gender as of culture. This space in-between does not feel like the cosmopolitanism or 'world citizenship' that some people have professed to belong to. Rather, it feels like a wound. But there is no way around that wound. The best I can do is make it visible and write about it.

My struggle with all of these issues is a very personal and individual one. But I also feel that it is the struggle of our times and our world. In a world of increasing migration, cultural interaction and international awareness, but increasingly one dominated by a new kind of colonialism, a neoliberal capitalist system that, without regard for any borders, swallows all of us up mercilessly, we are all constantly confronted with such questions of belonging and authenticity. The upsurge of nationalist and right-wing extremist voices in so many societies across the world speaks of this. So do the very vibrant and sometimes aggressive public debates on identity, belonging and cultural appropriation.

My partner expressed it best. Once, while he was talking to a relative in Pakistan on the phone, the relative asked about me, 'Vo vahanki hai?' Is she from over there (Germany)? My partner replied, 'Vo saari dunya ki paidavaar hai!' She is a product of the whole world! I loved that. Nothing has ever made me feel belonging as much as this Urdu sentence, whose nuances cannot be properly expressed in German or English. But, in the end, of course, we are all products of the whole world. We all have ancestors who came from somewhere else at some point in history and, in fact, if we go back far enough then we all descend from the same clan that originated in Africa and then ventured out to explore the Middle East and develop agriculture there.

We can barely imagine a life without inventions that were made millennia ago in what is today's Iraq, such as canalisation (even our word 'canal' is of Middle-Eastern origin), irrigation, cities and even bureaucracy. We all want to enjoy our originally South American tomatoes, potatoes and chocolate and a lot of us are quite dependent on the Ottoman invention of 'coffee' or the Chinese discovery of 'tea'. We all use the Chinese invention of paper, prefer to calculate with Arabic numbers and use an alphabet that, through Greek and Italian transmission, actually has its roots in modern Lebanon and the Sinai. And we all use words with Indian roots, such as 'shampoo', 'sugar', 'candy', 'orange', 'bungalow' and 'loot', while engaging with an English language which has half come from Germany and Denmark, the other half from France.

There is barely anything in our lives that has not come from somewhere else at some point. A lot of it was brought to us through ancient waves of immigration that we have already forgotten about but that has made us who we are; a lot of it was appropriated through a long history of colonial exploitation. It is important to understand that this multiple character of our existence which makes us all a 'product of the whole world' is also connected to histories of violence and power. It is equally important to recognise that we have inherited a global system fraught with structural violence and inequality and to recognise our privileges and responsibilities within this. Only by making this visible and engaging with it constantly can we be responsible citizens of the world.

3

EUNUCHS, SHEMALES, TRANSSEXUALS

THE USE OF GENDERED terms in early Muslim societies can help us understand the way in which today's gender identities and sexualities are culturally and historically contingent; first by tracing possible ancient connections between eunuchs and contemporary *khwajasara* and *hijra* communities; then by discovering the heritage of Mughal court eunuchs, which looms large in both the public imagination and the community's self-conception; and, finally, by pondering the issue of gendered vocabularies, and how the terms we use to describe gender and sexuality are contested and ever-changing. These are questions I've thought about a lot over the years.

I expect a few people to raise their eyebrows when encountering the title of this book. There may be a few Western transgender activists who say that by using the term 'eunuchs' I am buying into transphobic notions which imply that a trans woman can never be accepted as a 'real woman'. (Although this critique in itself would involve a potentially problematic conflation of trans women and *hijras*.) Trans exclusionary cisgender feminists might celebrate the title of this book for the same reasons.[1] A lot of South Asian LGBT activists might remark that by using the 'eunuch' trope I am falling back into a politically incorrect language that most of the English-speaking South Asian media has already abandoned. The irony is that, as already mentioned, the word now considered the politically correct word to use for transgender people in Pakistani Urdu, *khwajasara*, literally means nothing else but a court eunuch.

There is indeed an ancient connection between eunuchs and trans identities that has to be explored to properly understand the traditional self-image of the *khwajasara* and *hijra* community. This connection can arguably be traced back to the Mediterranean world, which we often consider to be the cradle of Western civilisation. We even find it referred to in the Bible. In the Gospel according to Matthew, Jesus says: 'For there are eunuchs, that were born so from their mother's womb: and there are eunuchs, that were made eunuchs by men: and there are eunuchs, that made themselves eunuchs for the kingdom of heaven's sake (19:12).' This verse often causes a considerable amount of confusion in the mind of today's reader. When we think of eunuchs, we usually think of castrated men. We may, for example, think of the young boys who were brutally emasculated by slave traders before being sold to the Ottomans for the purpose of serving at the harem of the Sultan in Istanbul. Or we may think of young boys who were brutally robbed of their manhood in sixteenth- to nineteenth-century Italy to preserve their pre-pubescent singing voices. But what are we to make of Jesus' remark that there are eunuchs that 'were born so from their mother's womb'?

In fact, during the lifetime of Jesus Christ and even long after that, the category of 'eunuch' appears to have been understood in a much broader sense than we often understand it today. A 'eunuch' was effectively almost everybody who was, in the eyes of society, neither a man nor a woman. Kathryn Ringrose notes that a compilation of Byzantine law outlined three different categories of eunuchs: *spadones*, who were born without ['male heterosexual'] sexual capabilities or desires; *thlibiai*, whose testicles had been crushed; and *kastratoi*, whose testicles had been removed.[2] Centuries after Jesus, then, the Eastern Mediterranean world still recognised a category of eunuchs who were 'born that way'. All of these eunuchs, whether born or made, were understood socially as a 'third gender'.

Apart from the categories mentioned above, the pre-Christian Mediterranean world also knew a number of people who had been assigned male at birth but later underwent ritual castration in the cause of a religious mystery cult and afterwards wore feminine dress, hair and make-up. The most famous of these were the *galloi* priests of the Anatolian goddess Kybele, whose cult centres could once be found from Asia to Great Britain and also, curiously, at a spot now occupied by the Vatican. The existence of these cults may have been why Jesus referred to 'eunuchs for the kingdom of heaven's sake' and while Christianity—and the Roman Catholic Church in particular—has in general only understood this statement as an endorsement of celibacy and monasticism, there have in the past been Christians who engaged in similar ritual castrations, most famously the Egyptian scholar Origen (third century) and the Russian Skoptsy movement (eighteenth to early twentieth century).

While we have often been instructed to think of the history of civilisation as one partitioned into 'East' and 'West', it is important to remember that Western Christendom and Islam both share their origins in the Eastern Mediterranean world that Jesus lived in and that was later occupied by the Byzantine Empire. In fact, early Muslim civilisation directly inherited from Byzantine civilisation in many ways. The Arab tribes that ventured to conquer much of the formerly Byzantine Middle East and North Africa region after the passing of their new Prophet Muhammad, peace be upon him and his family, were mostly nomadic, familiar with only a rudimentary urbanisation centred around small settlements like Makkah, which already had longstanding and strong trade relationships with Byzantium. After their first expansion, however, the early Muslims adopted much of Byzantine urban life. The Middle Eastern *hammam* is a direct descendant of Greco-Roman bathhouses. Early mosque architecture was an adaptation of the East Roman basilica. Muslims adopted food from Byzantine culture, as well as medicine and the natural sciences, which later, having been transmitted to the

West, became the basis for the European Renaissance and the Enlightenment. Another thing the Muslims adopted was the peculiar Byzantine institution of the court eunuch.

There has not, unfortunately, been enough research done on the continuities between Byzantine and early Muslim conceptions of the eunuch. The Arabs of the time of the Prophet were certainly aware of a category of castrated men that were referred to as *khasi*. They also knew other categories of people that were considered 'not fully male', although it is debatable as to whether they were understood as constituting a true 'third gender'. Amongst these were the *khuntha*, a person born with visibly intersex genitals, and the *mukhannath*, a person assigned male at birth but with feminine characteristics and behaviour, who would often dress up in feminine ways. It is worth noting that both words are closely related to each other. If we translate *khuntha* as 'intersex', then we could literally translate *mukhannath* as something like 'intersexified'. In some forms of modern colloquial Arabic, both words can be used interchangeably, although jurists of Muslim law have always been very careful about distinguishing between the *khuntha* and the *mukhannath*.

I will say a bit more about these genders of early Islam in the next chapter. But here let it suffice to say that both the *khuntha* and the *mukhannath* were integral parts of early Muslim society. Castration, on the other hand, was originally frowned upon by Muslims. There exists a famous saying of the Prophet Muhammad, peace be upon him and his family, that explicitly prohibits his followers from castrating people. Nevertheless, the influence of Byzantine culture on early Islam was so strong that Muslim monarchies started to adopt the institution of the 'court eunuch' with the help of a little ruse: the Prophet had prohibited creating castrated eunuchs but he had not explicitly prohibited owning castrated eunuchs. In fact, one of the wives of the Prophet, the Coptic Egyptian Maria, had had an Egyptian attendant who was a castrated eunuch. Muslim dynasties therefore started to purchase castrated slaves from non-Muslim neighbouring nations. A few European cities and city-states, notably Verdun and Venice, turned this into a very lucrative business.

At one particular point in early Islamic history, however, Muslim powers ventured to create castrated eunuchs for themselves. In the late seventh century, governors of the Umayyad dynasty started to persecute the *mukhannathun* (pl. of *mukhannath*), who had, until then, not been ostracised much. In the early eighth century, the Umayyad governor of Madinah ordered all *mukhannathun* of the Prophet's city to be castrated. In the *Kitab al-Aghani* (Book of Songs), however, tenth-century scholar al-Isfahani notes that many of the *mukhannathun* were not particularly horrified by this punishment. Some remarked, 'What would we do with an unused weapon anyway?' Here, for the first time in Islamic history, we have an account of the categories of the castrated eunuch and the born *mukhannath* being conflated.

In general, we are able to see that in medieval Muslim history castrated eunuchs were often seen as occupying a very similar gendered space to the *mukhannathun*. Shaun Marmon mentions that in the Mamluk period (thirteenth–sixteenth century), the eunuchs of the holy cities of Makkah and Madinah were often described with a sexually ambivalent language. He quotes the words of the judge 'Abd al-Wahhab al-Subki (d. 1355): 'When the eunuch mixes with women, he tells himself that he is a man, when he is with men, he tells himself that he is a woman.'[3] David Ayalon cites the scholar al-Tha'alibi (d. 1038), who remarked of the eunuchs at the Mamluk court in Egypt: 'They are described as being womanly and docile in bed at night and manly and warlike by day in a campaign and in similar circumstances.'[4] It seems almost as if al-Tha'alibi wants to say that eunuchs are the best companions for men in all situations!

In early modern times, this conflation of the categories of eunuch and *mukhannath* seems to have become almost standard.

In the Persian literature of the late medieval period we find that this conflation is also increasingly extended to the category of the intersex *khuntha*. The famous thirteenth-century Persian poet Rumi, for example, repeatedly uses the word *mukhannas* (the Persian and Urdu pronunciation of the Arabic *mukhannath*) to mean *khuntha* as well. In documents of Mughal India, the eunuch as such, whether 'born' or 'made', is also often merely referred to as *mukhannas*, while the word *khwajasara* is explicitly only used for eunuchs employed in the royal court. *Khwajasara* was therefore chiefly the name of a specific appointment, while *mukhannas* was employed for the broad range of people that were chosen for this appointment. There is still a mosque in the North Indian city of Agra, famed for the Taj Mahal, that is known as the *Masjid-e Mukhannasan*, 'the mosque of the *mukhannas*'. It was reportedly built on the orders of the Mughal emperor Akbar (sixteenth century), for an especially pious court eunuch of his, whose prayers for rain at times of drought were always answered. Subsequently, it was used as the special mosque of the eunuchs of Agra.

Very early on in the history of early modern Muslim South Asia, the categories of 'castrated eunuch' and *mukhannas* were also conflated with the native category of the *hijra*. In some of the earliest Urdu dictionaries we can already find an equation between the words *khunsa*, *mukhannas*, *khasi*, *khwajasara* and, eventually, *hijra*, with *hijra* soon becoming by far the most well-known colloquial word to encompass all of these categories, having the same breadth of meaning as Jesus' use of the word 'eunuch'. In fact, just as in ancient antiquity in the Eastern Mediterranean, in common early modern South Asian understanding there seemed to be no need to clearly distinguish between these categories; all were human beings that fell outside of the usual gender binary and who were seen as neither men nor women. Further conflation of categories can be observed in the dictionaries of the later colonial age. In John Thompson Platts' *Dictionary of Urdu, Classical Hindi and English* (1884), for example, the verb *mukhannas karnaa* is directly translated as 'to emasculate', although being a *mukhannas* is not necessarily identified with being castrated.

This conflation of categories irritates and frustrates us today. How could Jesus, the Byzantines, early modern Muslims and pre-colonial and colonial South Asians be so imprecise as to mix up categories such as castrated men, intersex people and transgender individuals? Our belief in historical progress sometimes makes us think that the explanation for this confusion can only be the unenlightened attitudes of the past. But I have also in recent years often been told by Pakistani transgender activists that it is frustrating to have to constantly educate the public on the differences between being transgender and being intersex, because the mentioned 'confusion' is still so ingrained in South Asian thinking.

But we need to understand that this 'confusion' is actually no confusion at all but merely the product of a very different way of thinking about gender. Both Byzantine Christian and later Muslim ideas on gender were rooted partly in a Hellenistic understanding according to which the original human being had been androgynous and had only been differentiated by gendered categories later. Some of that androgyny was still present in each human being and different bodily fluids, called 'humours', had an influence on how it would be expressed. In some societies it was also believed that children were to some extent androgynous and rituals such as male circumcision (and also female genital mutilation) were originally understood to reduce some of that androgyny in order to create a more defined gender. Castrated eunuchs, intersex people and people we may now read as transgender were all considered 'less defined' in very similar ways and it was assumed that their humours were very similar.

This kind of social construction of gender may seem very strange to us today, where gender is mostly seen as very binary, either defined by a clear 'biological sex' visible in genitals and/or chromosomes, or an innate gender identity, or a combination of both. But our own social construction of gender is also very inconsistent. Intersex people in particular constantly challenge us on the meaning of our binary categories of 'biological sex'. We increasingly ask whether homosexual and transgender people were 'born this way' or not, which is essentially a question about their biology. Many LGBT activists in particular, but also its most severe opponents, have become quite obsessed with that particular question which ultimately shares the very same concerns with the traditional South Asian 'confusion' about intersex and transgender issues.

In fact, the obsession with that question has led to the search for the 'gay gene' and some transgender activists claiming that transsexuality is a form of 'brain intersexuality'. And, in fact, since our modern term 'intersexuality' embraces a lot of different variations in genitals, secondary sex characteristics, chromosomes and hormones, some scientists have made the argument that transsexuality and homosexuality are also in some ways 'intersex'. Equally, there exists a considerable overlap between intersex and transgender populations: I personally know more than one person who considered themselves to be a transgender woman assigned male at birth, who was diagnosed with the intersex Klinefelter syndrome later in life. We, therefore, have to admit that our own gender categories are often at least as blurry and arbitrary as older categories and leave just as many questions open.

Some Western researchers have become preoccupied with trying to neatly separate 'native Indian' categories of gender from Muslim categories of gender. It has been suggested that the *hijra gharanas* are rooted mostly in South Asian pre-Muslim history and that the courtly *khwajasaras* originally may not have had much to do with the *hijra gharanas*. This view has been enthusiastically adopted by some Hindu nationalist LGBT activists in India today. But it explicitly clashes with the narratives of some of the most prestigious *hijra gharanas* both in India and Pakistan. The *gharana* whose *deras* I stayed in during the early 2000s has a very well-documented 'pedigree' that traces itself back in an initiatory line directly to the eunuchs of the royal Mughal court. Other *gharanas*, both in India and Pakistan, have very similar 'pedigrees', although it is part of the strict rules of the *hijra* system to not mention the names of the dead to outsiders and therefore *hijras* rarely have an interest in publishing these pedigrees in order to satisfy the nosiness of the outside world.

There was one prominent case, however, where a *hijra gharana* of Delhi decided to disclose some of its documents in order to gain custody of an historical building that once belonged to the community of royal eunuchs: the *'hijron ka khanqah'*, a Muslim shrine and burial ground in South Delhi's Mehrauli dating back to the fifteenth century. It has been in the custody of the *hijras* of Delhi's Turkoman Gate since the first half of the twentieth century, after they proved in court that they were direct lineal descendants of the Mughal eunuchs who had been the previous custodians of the cemetery.

It is true that not all *hijra gharanas* have such initiatory lines leading back to the royal Muslim courts. Some are more closely connected to the temple of the Hindu goddess Bahuchara Mata in Gujarat, for example, who has long been considered to be the patron goddess of *hijras* in North Indian Hinduism. There are some interesting parallels between the cult of Bahuchara Mata and the Greco-Roman worship of the aforementioned Anatolian goddess Kybele, the most obvious being the symbolism of the rooster. In Roman art, the rooster appears as a symbol of the cult of Kybele, the Greek name of Kybele's eunuch priests, *galloi*, often equated with the Latin word for roosters, *galli*, while

Bahuchara Mata is always depicted riding on a rooster. It is not completely unimaginable that some of the Gujarati *hijra gharanas* could possibly have origins in the Hellenistic cult of Kybele. The Hellenistic world did once stretch as far as modern-day Punjab after all and the ports of ancient Gujarat did have trade relationships with the Roman Empire.

In the traditional histories of many *khwajasara gharanas*, however, the notion that *khwajasaras* and *hijras* descend from the courtly eunuchs employed by Muslim dynasties of North India between the eleventh and the early twentieth century—eunuchs were employed by Muslim royals in Hyderabad until it was forcibly integrated into the Indian Union in 1948—is most favoured. After all, eunuchs occupied positions of great political importance and were highly respected socially. As late as 1832, we read in the memoirs of Mrs Meer Hassan Ali:

> [The eunuchs] are in great request among the highest order of people ... [They] are generally faithfully attached to the interest and welfare of their employer; they are much in the confidence of their master and mistress, and very seldom betray their trust. ... [They] are admitted at all hours and seasons to the zeenahnahs [the harems]; and often, by the liberality of their patrons, become rich and honourable. In Oude [Awadh] there have been many instances of Eunuchs arriving to great honour, distinctions, and vast possessions.[5]

There is much to suggest that the worlds of pre-Muslim *hijra* lineages and Muslim court eunuchs started to intersect at an early stage. The Mughals often bought castrated slaves, just as other contemporary Muslim dynasties such as the Ottomans did. But there are a lot of indications that they also recruited some of their eunuchs from the local *hijra* communities. There are also several cases of prominent eunuchs in Mughal and post-Mughal Indian history who are very specifically described as 'born eunuchs' and not castrated slaves. Many of these 'born eunuchs' often came from impoverished families who gave their children to the royal courts in the hope that they would find a profitable career there. One of the most famous of these 'born eunuchs' was a certain Almas Ali Khan who became the leading court eunuch in the Kingdom of Awadh in the late eighteenth century, under the rule of Nawab Asaf ud-Daula and his mother Bahu Begum. Almas Ali Khan has often been described as the most powerful person in the kingdom after the *nawab* and his mother and his influence in Awadh is especially remembered by the *hijras* of Lucknow, even to this day. A number of other famous 'born eunuchs' have been mentioned in the works of the history of Awadh and it seems that Almas Ali Khan himself preferred for 'born eunuchs' to be employed at the court of Awadh instead of castrated slaves.

I have been taught in my *dera* that 'born eunuchs', understood as either intersex or transgender people, were always preferred for service in the private chambers of the rulers. I have found no documented proof of this, but it does make sense: kings may not have felt safe having castrated men around their women, even if they were unable to sire children. Choosing someone who appeared feminine by nature and who expressed no romantic or sexual interest in their women was a much safer option. Today, of course, we would not say that such characteristics are necessarily possessed by intersex people and transgender women; at that time, however, gender expression and sexuality were considered more closely related to each other (more on this point in Chapter 7).

Jessica Hinchy, historian of *hijra* and *khwajasara* communities under colonial British rule, notes a curious incident that happened after the British invasion of the Kingdom of Awadh in 1856. Victorian British officers were especially worried about the morals of the Muslim aristocracy of Awadh and its capital city Lucknow. The last *nawab* had a reputation of being overly dedicated to the pleasures of life—even though he was reportedly loved by almost all of his subjects—and the Muslim aristocracy in general had a reputation of being decadent and morally corrupt. There was much that horrified the British when it came to the lifestyle of Awadh's Muslim aristocracy but few things horrified them as much as the institution of employing eunuchs as servants in their private homes. To the Victorian British these eunuchs appeared a threat to the ideals of family and sexuality they were preaching.

At one point, British officials ordered a medical examination of all of the eunuch servants of Awadh. To their great shock, and contrary to their expectations, they discovered that a large number of these servants had not been castrated at all. Many of these eunuch servants had been mere 'male transvestites' as the British labelled them, or *zenanas*. The British were horrified to realise that the Muslim aristocracy, who had given these servants full access to the female quarters of their private homes, had never even bothered to enquire about what they considered the unquestionably male biology of the servants. In fact, it seems that to South Asian Muslims of that time being a 'eunuch' was never so much a physical or biological matter but mostly one of gender expression.

Hinchy meticulously traces the development of legal discrimination against *hijras* and *khwajasaras* under British colonial rule in the nineteenth century, documenting the devastating effect that the passing of the 1871 Criminal Tribes Act had on these communities. This law had the explicit goal of exterminating all eunuch societies of South Asia. The British government criminalised both the court eunuchs and the *hijras* that went out to bless people on *badhai*. Persecution was at times brutal, with many *hijras* and *khwajasaras* dying in colonial prisons and many *hijra* households destroyed. While the *badhai-hijras* could often still escape the control of British authorities, colonial laws left all court eunuchs in regions that had fallen directly under British jurisdiction—including Awadh since 1856—unemployed and impoverished. Some former court eunuchs may in this situation have sought refuge with the *badhai-hijras*. It is my theory that it is in this situation that the lineages of the royal courtly eunuchs and the *badhai-hijras* eventually got entangled with each other.

It should be noted that not only do Indian and Pakistani *khwajasaras* and *hijras* often present themselves as descendants of royal court eunuchs but in the public imagination of mainstream society they are also seen as such. Indian and Pakistani cinema and television has contributed much to the construction of this public imagination. For example, both in the classic film epic *Mughal-e-Azam* (1960) and in the more recent movie *Jodha Akbar* (2008), the court eunuchs of Mughal emperor Akbar are depicted as stereotypical *hijras* wearing female clothes. Stereotypical *hijras* also appear as eunuch attendants in Islamicate settings in Muzaffar Ali's offbeat movie *Anjuman* (1986), in the religious movie *Niyaz aur Namaaz* (1977) and even in the popular Indian children's series *Mullah Nasruddin* (1990). We find the same in Pakistani historical fantasy soap *Mor Mahal* (2016), where the main eunuch is played by the brilliant Ali Saleem, better known as Pakistan's most famous drag queen, TV presenter Begum Nawazish Ali. Even in international co-productions *hijras* often appear in a clearly Islamicate setting connecting them with the royal eunuchs of Muslim aristocracy. In *Heat and Dust* (1983), for example, a group of *hijras* appear to sing and dance at the court of a Muslim *nawab* to entertain his English lover. In Jamil Dehlavi's *Immaculate Conception* (1992), on the other hand, Pakistani eunuch custodians of a Muslim shrine dazzle a British-American Jewish couple in the wake of the Salman Rushdie affair.

Despite this perceived historical continuity, both in the private histories of many *hijra gharanas* and in India and Pakistan's public perception, during the two past decades of my engagement with

South Asian *hijra* and *khwajasara* communities, the English label 'eunuch' has faded into the background while other more modern and internationally recognised representational terms have made their introduction.

One of the more curious terms to be popularised has been the word 'shemale'. Westerners mostly know of this term thanks to the porn industry; 'shemale pornography' is one of the most popular forms of pornography worldwide. Whilst the past popularity of this term in South Asia may be related to its prevalent use in pornography, it must be said that from the mid-2000s onwards the word was used as a self-designation by many Pakistani *khwajasaras* in particular. It was *khwajasara* guru and activist Almas Bobby, well-known for several appearances on television and her role in Pakistani movie *Bol* (2011), who vigorously championed the use of the term 'shemale' for a time. Since then, the word 'shemale' has even appeared as an official English translation of '*khwajasara*' on government forms where people are asked to specify gender and I have, on more than one occasion, been asked by Pakistani policemen whether I was 'female or shemale'. In more recent years, however, the international NGO scene has taught Pakistani *khwajasaras* that 'shemale' is not an appropriate self-referent and since then the term 'transgender' has become popularised.

I still somewhat mourn the passing of the word shemale. Back in 1994, transgender activist Kate Bornstein pointed out in her innovative work *Gender Outlaw: on Men, Women, and the Rest of Us* that preferences for specific vocabularies describing trans experiences were often very much marked by social and economic class. Working-class transgender women, many of them sex-workers—and the original activists of our communities, long before middle-class LGBT people dared to join them—often saw no issue in referring to themselves proudly and publicly as she-males, queens or trannies. Of course, these same words were often used as insults by cisgender, heterosexual people as well. But the same could, after all, also be said about words such as 'gay' or 'queer', words that were also re-appropriated very confidently by the community and are now used in an empowering way by many designated as such. It is often middle-class transgender women, however, who feel that these words can only be understood in belittling and discriminatory ways. This has now become the mainstream opinion in all Western transgender movements, an opinion which has successfully been taught to other people around the world.

The word 'transgender' itself, as much as the conceptions attached to it, also has its own contested history in the Western LGBT movement and beyond and should never be seen as a natural choice. It has its roots in the efforts of the German-Jewish sexologist Dr Magnus Hirschfeld who, in Berlin in the early twentieth century, was one of the first people to introduce such words as 'transvestit' and 'transsexuell' to the public. Interestingly, Hirschfeld's conception of sexuality and gender was very different from that of the LGBT movement of the later twentieth century which adopted and improved his vocabulary. For Hirschfeld, the people he labelled 'transvestiten' and 'transsexuelle' (most of whom we would identify as transgender now), as much as homosexual and bisexual men and women, belonged to a continuum beyond, or rather between, the two binary genders. Hirschfeld, who himself identified as a homosexual man, first published some of his ideas in 1904 in a book entitled *Berlins Drittes Geschlecht* ('The Third Gender of Berlin'). It should be noted that Hirschfeld's ideas were inspired by anthropological data gathered from all over the world during the colonial age and that one of Hirschfeld's closest associates was Hugo Hamid Marcus, a Polish-German Jew who had converted to Islam.

Hamid Marcus was active in Berlin's slowly growing Muslim community of the 1920s and was affiliated with the Wilmersdorf

Mosque which, through its organisational origins in the Lahore Ahmadiyya movement, had strong ties to South Asia and to the Woking Mosque in the UK. Marcus did not seem to see much conflict between his Muslim religion and community engagement and his very vocal fight for the rights of sexual minorities. In fact, he himself was also very vocal about being homosexual. Without the Lahore Ahmadiyya movement, this may have been a source of internal conflict for him. But as this missionary movement strove to present Islam as a modern, enlightened and progressive faith, these conflicts never came too much to the fore. Persecuted by the Nazis, Marcus fled to Switzerland in 1939, where he passed away in 1966.

Ever since Magnus Hirschfeld's definitions, the meanings of terms such as 'transvestite', 'transsexual' and 'transgender' have changed constantly and each generation has led fiery new debates on the correct vocabulary with which trans issues should be described, along with the correct theories backing such vocabulary. What I find astonishing, and also quite worrying, is that in the course of my lifetime many of these debates have only become even more dogmatic and essentialising in character. The early LGBT community still allowed a certain amount of fluidity between different LGBT identities. And in the 1990s, activists such as Kate Bornstein were largely arguing for a dynamic understanding of both what it means to be a woman and what it means to be trans.

Some of that more dynamic understanding has in the years leading up to 2020 returned in the form of new identities, such as non-binary, genderfluid or genderqueer. But many transgender women in particular have become more and more insistent on very narrow conceptions of gender and sexuality. I have witnessed very vicious wars of words, for example, between women who insist that 'transgender' is the only correct word and women who insist that 'transsexual' is the only correct word, even though in the end both camps mean essentially the same thing. I have also witnessed arguments between people who insist that being transgender is always fundamentally a non-binary experience and others who insist that one cannot be transgender if one does not identify clearly with one of the binary genders.

There is also a tendency in some circles of the trans activist world to insist that all people in all phases of history and in all cultures who were assigned male at birth but understood and presented themselves in feminine ways should be properly labelled as transgender women. These activists would consider it an affront that I do not call Kybele's *galloi* priests priestesses and that I prefer to use the male pronoun for several historical *mukhannathun* and 'born eunuchs', even though from what we know, *galloi*, *mukhannathun* and 'born eunuchs' seemed mostly to have used the male pronoun for themselves and did not understand themselves as women. I would argue that there is an implicitly colonial assumption of historical progress in the minds of these activists: how people in other periods of history or in other cultures whom *we* would call transgender expressed themselves and named themselves does not matter at all, since it is we who have the true knowledge of how a transgender person is supposed to feel and be represented.

A couple of years ago, I had a conversation with a trans activist from the US, who was in the process of getting prepared to do research in Pakistan. Before starting any of that research, she claimed that *khwajasaras* and *hijras* must have always considered themselves to be women, and that it was only due to the oppression of a patriarchal society that they were not able to express themselves properly and had started to use a language describing themselves as 'eunuchs' or 'third gender'. But that is very clearly not true. The *hijras* that I lived with in the early 2000s were very clear in voicing their opinion that they did not want to be seen as women, with a self-confidence I have never seen in Western transgender circles. They were also very clear about the theory behind that opinion; it was not merely a matter of expression. They had a complex way of thinking about gender and sexuality that was internally consistent, even if it did not agree with now-popular globalised Western notions. They were highly aware of the meaning of their gender in this world and its place in life.

For many of us Western trans women, coming from centuries of binary assumptions about gender leads us to believe that not being seen as a 'real woman' automatically implies that our gender is not taken seriously and that we are either seen as 'transvestite men' or just simply as freaks. In fact, this is often how trans exclusionary feminists depict transgender women. It is this experience which seems to cause the kind of discomfort expressed by the trans activist mentioned above. The old gurus would, however, never feel such a discomfort. The traditional views of *hijras* and *khwajasaras* on themselves—that they are a 'third gender' that owes its inherent value to God and does not need any validation from cisgender men or women—is expressed with self-confidence. This 'third' carries a femininity and sexuality that, to some extent, has a strong connection with the female experience. But it has, nevertheless, been given an identity and spiritual power by the Divine that is very specific to it and which cannot be owned by anybody else.

I have certainly seen a shift not only in vocabulary but also in the expression of this idea over the two decades that I have worked with the community. Younger generations are indeed often influenced by more globalised notions of gender and sexuality and increasingly incorporate versions of these ideas into their own identity formation, for instance referring to themselves as 'transgender women'. More recently, some have started to use terms such as 'non-binary'. But many of the older gurus are still very insistent that equating *khwajasaras* with women is a fundamentally wrong idea. In their eyes, it is not they who are unable to express themselves properly, but it is the Western transgender woman who is deluded.

An obvious question to come up in the reader's mind is whether I believe that these older gurus are right or not. I will elaborate in detail on that question in Chapter 6 of this book. But here let me just say that I find it an important thing to acknowledge that gender identity can apparently be experienced in very different ways, depending on social and cultural context and, as we have seen, it is very much dependent on our histories, individual histories as much as collective ones. In my opinion, there is no absolute 'right' or 'wrong' in these matters. My ideal is an open conversation that has space for multiple positions.

It always astonishes me how often people, of many different gender identities, sexual orientations, religious identities and cultures, are often so completely convinced that their particular way of experiencing and understanding gender and sexuality is the only true and correct one and that everybody else is either just deluded, ignorant or blinded by false social expectations. The sheer presence of a boundless diversity of ever-changing and constantly shifting expressions of gender and sexuality throughout human history blatantly exposes such naive convictions as illusions.

4

THE GENDERS OF ISLAM

THERE WAS A MOMENT during one of my stays in a *dera* in Delhi in the early 2000s when I was supposed to return to Germany soon and feeling quite distraught about it. Later on, I would develop a more balanced view of the issues of marginalisation and discrimination that my sisters in South Asia faced in their everyday life. At that point, however, I had seen much more visibility and everyday acceptance of transgender people in South Asia than in Europe. While I was astonished that in India many people thought that I had powers to bless and curse others, in European society I believed I was merely seen as a freak with little agency to defend myself against assaults. I told one of the older grandmother gurus at my *dera* about my feelings and also shared with her accounts of one or two transphobic experiences that I had experienced in Germany. She said to me, 'You know, child, whatever people say or do to you, never forget that you belong to the people who hold the keys to the holy Ka'aba in Makkah and to the mosque of the Prophet, may peace be upon him and his family, in Madinah.'

I was deeply touched, and utterly surprised, by her words. I had read that from the thirteenth century until the early twentieth century, Makkah and Madinah, the holiest places of Islam, had always been guarded and maintained by a society of eunuchs. In the previous chapter, I quoted the fourteenth-century scholar and jurist 'Abd al-Wahhab al-Subki, who said that these eunuchs of the holy cities seemed to express themselves as interchangeably male and female. I had often wondered whether there had been any ancient connection between the Indian *hijra* community and these eunuchs of the holy places—especially since I had also read that from the fifteenth to the eighteenth century most of the eunuchs of the holy cities were recruited from India. But I had not expected that the *hijra* community itself would have preserved some knowledge of this connection. I had underestimated the accuracy of the community's oral tradition.

To many Muslims today, perhaps even more so those who do not have a South Asian background, the idea that there could be any connection between the guardians of the most holy places of Islam and a society of Indian transgender and intersex people must seem quite absurd. A lot of the things that were once taken for granted in the Muslim world for centuries, however, now seem absurd to Muslims today. Scholars such as Ali Ghandour, Shahab Ahmed, Olivier Roy and Thomas Bauer have written extensively on the huge gap that separates the religious and cultural experiences of Muslims in the twenty-first and twentieth centuries from the worlds of their predecessors. The importance that eunuchs once held, both in the secular and the religious life of Muslim societies, is one thing that has been left behind.

Some Muslims still remember these old connections, however, even in the land of the holy cities. In 2007, a few years before public discussion on the status of *khwajasaras* and *hijras* in India and Pakistan was to take off, an *Arab News* journalist bumped into a group of Indian *hijras* performing the pilgrimage to Makkah and who introduced themselves to him as 'being neither men nor women'. The journalist immediately made the connection between these *hijras* and the eunuchs of the holy places, who were never directly addressed with the descriptive word *khasi* but always with the Arabic title *aghawaat*. The journalist wondered what Saudi religious authorities, stereotypically known for not being very tolerant of the diversity of local religious phenomena in the Muslim world in general, and sexual diversity in particular, would say about these *hijras*. He asked *Arab News'* Islamic Affairs Editor, the Muslim scholar Adil Salahi, for advice and quoted him as saying:

If the eunuch is a man who has been castrated, all the rulings concerning men apply to him. If it is a question of a person being created thus, then whatever the person appears to be applies to him. If the eunuch says he is a man, or if he says he is a woman, Islam accepts this from him in things which do not give him any material advantage. As far as pilgrimage [sic], the eunuch is required to offer the pilgrimage just as everyone else. If the eunuch's form suggests he is a man, such as having hair in the face, then he is a man. If the form suggests a woman, such as having breasts, then she is a woman.[1]

Adil Salahi's reply may at first seem unexpected from a Saudi Muslim scholar, but his reply very much belongs to a long line of traditional Muslim thinking. This is a line that on the one hand holds space for the existence of people who do not neatly fit into a clearly defined gender binary, but on the other hand has always struggled to determine ways in which such people could fit into the different requirements canonical Islamic law sometimes has when it comes to the religious duties of men and women. Neither the *Arab News* journalist nor the Muslim scholar, however, seemed to be much confused by the presence of eunuchs at the Hajj. The *hijras* from Bhopal also told the journalist that in general they faced no issues during their pilgrimage: 'Nobody bothered us nor did we bother anybody.'[2] On one occasion when fellow pilgrims were not comfortable with their presence, they were given their own separate room. Otherwise, they did not experience any problems.

Indeed, the Hajj has for a long time been an important part of *hijra* and *khwajasara* culture and in many ways performing the pilgrimage has traditionally been one of the most important steps to becoming an influential and respected guru. Our aforementioned grandmother guru also informed me that the pilgrimage has often offered an occasion through which to maintain relationships with the *aghawaat* of Madinah. In 2013, as Saudi photographer Adel al-Quraishi portrayed in his series 'The

Guardians', an old generation of eunuchs still guarded the Prophet Muhammad's (p.b.u.h.) burial chamber in the holy city. Our grandmother guru claimed that she had connected with them on each of her three pilgrimages to the holy cities. In fact, she claimed that there had been longstanding connections between her *gharana* and the eunuchs of Madinah for many generations, going back to Mughal times.

In al-Quraishi's portrait photography, there is a certain softness and femininity to the eunuchs of Madinah. But they are dressed in an official outfit that probably harks back to Ottoman times, giving them an air of very masculine authority. They look quite different from most Indian *hijras* who would usually wear make-up and dress up in colourful feminine *shalwar kameez* or saris. After her last Hajj, however, our grandmother guru had also stopped dressing up in an explicitly feminine way, wearing no make-up or jewellery but only simple white clothes which made her look quite androgynous. I could very much imagine her in the official uniform of a eunuch of Madinah.

It is partly this old connection to the eunuchs of the holy cities that gives the traditional *hijras* and *khwajasaras* of South Asia a deep sense of belonging to Islam. It should be said at this point that not every *hijra* or *khwajasara* is a practising Muslim. There are many *hijras* in India who come from Hindu households and, as I have already mentioned, some of the Indian *gharanas* have longstanding connections to specific Hindu temples, such as the temple of Bahuchara Mata in Gujarat. In Pakistan, I have often come across Christian *khwajasaras* and, as recently as 2020, a lovely female pastor from Karachi, Ghazala Shafique, has opened a church specifically for the Christian *khwajasara* community. A lot of the most traditional *gharanas*, both in India and Pakistan, do however understand themselves as 'institutionally Muslim'. That means that in those *gharanas* an initiation is always accompanied by a conversion to Islam. This has been observed in Gayatri Reddy's ethnography on the *hijras* of Hyderabad.[3] One of the chapters of that work is entitled 'We are all Muslim now', a quote from one of the *hijras* Reddy had interviewed, referring to the fact that every *hijra* in her house had to nominally become Muslim. In fact, even in 1823, Alex Burnes, a Lieutenant in the colonial British army in Bombay, informs us in a piece called *Eunuchs or Pawyus of Cutch*: 'All Pawyus [a local word for *hijras*] are Mahommedans.'[4]

This nominal conversion to Islam is a remnant, it seems, of the nominal conversion that each eunuch once had to undergo when entering the society of royal eunuchs in the aristocratic courts of the past. Such a conversion does not necessarily affect all of the existing religious convictions and practices of the initiated *hijra*. Many *hijras* who come from Hindu family backgrounds often still engage in some of the same overlapping and complementary practices as *hijras* from Muslim backgrounds, something once very typical of many layers of Indian society. Even after their Hajj, for example, they may still pray at the shrines of Bahuchara Mata and other Hindu deities. In any case, their conversion gives them a sense of connection to the royal eunuchs of the past that is understood to be prestigious and beneficial, albeit less so in an increasingly Hindu nationalist India. There are many *hijras* however, even those of Hindu origin, who are very devout Muslims, especially in old age.

In the house right across from the little Friday mosque, the *dera* I described at the beginning of the Introduction, this devotion was especially visible due to the active participation of several *hijras* in the religious life of the larger Muslim community. Several of the *hijras*, myself included, regularly took part in the Friday prayers of the mosque. For Friday prayers as much as for Hajj, *hijras* traditionally remove all jewellery and dress up in simple androgynous white clothes. When I have spoken about this in front of audiences in the West, I have often been asked

87

whether this was an act of hiding their true gender identity. It was, however, never understood as anything of the sort in the community. After all, everybody in the little village around the mosque knew the *hijras* personally. There was no hiding. It was simply considered the appropriate dress, in order to not distract the men from their prayers. The gurus often arranged for huge pots of biryani to be cooked on Fridays and, after the prayers, this biryani was always distributed to the poor of the neighbourhood, thus fulfilling another important duty of a good Muslim, that of always taking care of those in need. The *hijras* were known as pious and generous within that little village community and the *imam* of the mosque often came over to have friendly discussions with the older gurus.

In those days, no-one in the Muslim societies I interacted with in India and Pakistan seemed to doubt that *hijras* were simply *hijras*. There was not much else to think about their existence. They were a part of God's creation and for the losses and pains they endured—being ostracised by their birth families; being unable to take part in heterosexual married life and create biological families—God had recompensed them with special spiritual powers. Even more so, people knew that they had a privileged connection to the Muslim past and therefore many ordinary Muslims often saw them as reminders of better times in the Islamic world. *Hijras* had not yet achieved an official legal status in India or Pakistan and there was no visible *hijra* and *khwajasara* activism. The world of *hijras* was confined to traditional *gharanas* and *deras*, a world which still held many secrets and which wider society associated with scandalous stories, passed on as rumours and gossip but which nobody actually wanted to explore. Larger society kept a respectful distance from the *hijra* community, a distance which could sometimes breed discrimination and misunderstanding but which in many ways also functioned to protect the community.

Within the community, the older gurus struggled to keep an old Islamicate ethos alive. They preached against the eating of non-halal meat and the drinking of alcohol, against sex work and too much romancing, but they were rarely very successful with that—in part because everybody knew that they themselves had not been very strict about those things in their younger years. They also struggled to keep the old lore of the community alive. Televisions had already invaded every *dera*, then the internet arrived along with the first mobile phones. The younger generations grew up in an increasingly neoliberal capitalist society that had become more aggressively Hindu. Not many of the young *hijras* were interested in the old lore. I was, of course. But the old gurus knew that I would never occupy any prominent position in the community. This was not because I was a foreigner and could not settle down there but simply because it quickly became clear to them that I had too many battles of my own to fight with the old hierarchies and rules.

I kept plenty of notes on the stories the gurus had to share, however. I was always astonished by the depth of their knowledge. Many had originally come from very humble backgrounds. The above-mentioned grandmother guru, for example, had come to Delhi from a poor rural background during the last decades of the British Raj. She could still remember the occupying British army and there may have been only two or three generations separating her from eunuchs who had served the last Mughal emperor, Bahadur Shah Zafar, who died in exile in 1862. She could read and write some Urdu but had received little formal education. Nevertheless, she carried a wealth of knowledge on the history of her community, the teachings of the Quran, the sayings of the Prophet and the teachings of other religious communities in her heart.

When she admonished me to always remember that I belonged to the same community that held the keys to the mosque of the Prophet, she also shared a number of other teachings with me that, to her, proved the elevated rank of *hijras* in the teachings of true Islam. She pointed out, for example, that the Quran emphasises that the angels were neither male nor female. Were we not as well, therefore, somewhat similar to the angels? I wondered whether the *imam* from the nearby mosque would think her words blasphemous. But grandmother did not seem to think so. She continued to remind me that many of the deities worshipped by the Hindus were also, effectively, *hijras*.

Shiva had castrated himself, after all, and hence his severed phallus has been worshipped as the holy *shivalingam*. Shiva also often appeared as Ardhanarishvara, in a form that merges the male and the female. Krishna had once appeared in female form, as Mohini. Even the otherwise very masculine hero Arjuna once had to spend several years of his life as a *hijra*. Another hero of the Hindu Mahabharata, Shikhandi, was also known to have been a *hijra*. For grandmother guru all these figures occupied a place in her Muslim universe as well. Not as deities, of course, but as pious human beings of the past. In that regard, her views of Hindu deities like Krishna were very similar to those of respected Indian Muslim scholars and intellectuals such as Mirza Mazhar Jan-e Janan or Maulana Hasrat Mohani, only they had an added transgender twist!

I was also astonished to find out that she shared a Quranic interpretation of Surah 4, aptly named 'The Women', with modern feminist interpreters of the holy book. The first verse says, 'O humankind, fear your Lord, who created you from one single soul and created from her its partner and from both of them many men and women.' Grandmother insisted that this meant that the original human being, the original Adam, had been androgynous and that all genders were eventually rooted in that original androgyny. Indeed, I later found out that some Muslim thinkers of the past had also connected the notion found in this verse with the well-known story from Plato's *Symposium*, in which the original human beings had once been spherical creatures whom Zeus had separated into two bodies which now populate in the form of heterosexual and homosexual couples constantly in search of their other half.

Grandmother guru's localised Islamicate knowledge fit very well into a wider world of Muslim knowledge on the validity of genders beyond the binary. This knowledge once existed on many different social levels in almost all Muslim majority regions of the world. It should be mentioned, however, that the pre-colonial Muslim past was not a paradise of sexual freedom and unlimited gender expression. Such ideas, sometimes taught by queer Muslim activists today, are as wrong as ideas of an essentialised Islam that has always been sexually repressive. However, there have been periods when there was indeed a much more widely accepted diversity of sexualities and genders across the Muslim world and when many Muslim societies had space for those who did not fit the gender binary.

We have already mentioned the *mukhannathun* of early Arab Muslim societies and it is worth noting that these people, who are often referred to as 'effeminates' in English-language academic literature, were once seen as a pretty normal part of these societies. Everett K. Rowson was one of the first scholars to present us with a study on the presence of the *mukhannathun* in the city of the Prophet in the early centuries of Islamic history.[5] What we can gather from Rowson's work is that even though there were periods in this history of greater and lesser acceptance of the *mukhannathun*—they experienced forms of persecution in the Umayyad times in particular—there was never a period in early Muslim history in which the *mukhannathun* had not been a constant presence in society. These *mukhannathun* were always described as human beings who were assigned male at birth and used male pronouns but who acted and dressed in feminine-coded ways, often adopting glamorous names such as 'Tuways' ('little peacock'). They were famed as singers, dancers or comedians and therefore were often required as entertainers on celebratory occasions. Sometimes they were seen as the perfect go-betweens to arrange marriages between men and women.

Interestingly, while in later centuries *mukhannathun* (and also *hijras*) were mostly imagined as being exclusively sexually attracted to men, these early *mukhannathun* expressed heterosexual, homosexual and probably bisexual desires. We know of early *mukhannathun* who were married to cisgender women and had children by them. Traditions from the times of the Prophet, however, indicate that Islam had more issues with *mukhannathun* who voiced a sexual interest in women than those only attracted to men. A particularly well-known tradition describes how a *mukhannath* used to regularly visit the wives of the Prophet Muhammad (p.b.u.h.) before the Prophet realised that he had an eye for female beauty and heard him describe it in shameful ways, henceforth prohibiting these visits. The Quran in Surah 24 Ayah 31 also mentions a category of 'male servants without male desires', in whose presence Muslim women are allowed to show themselves in the same free way as in front of other women. Early commentators often remarked that this category included *mukhannathun* without any sexual inclination towards women. In South Asia, Muslim scholars have traditionally also identified this category with *hijras* and *khwajasaras*.

Scott Siraj al-Haqq Kugle has adeptly demonstrated that this one incident of the Prophet prohibiting a particular *mukhannath* from visiting his wives has given birth to a whole range of fairly spurious traditions claiming that the Prophet had a general dislike or even hatred of *mukhannathun*.[6] It is quite likely that these traditions emerged during the periods of Umayyad rule in which *mukhannathun* were persecuted and forcibly castrated. In modern times, Muslim scholars have often used these traditions to support a transphobic and homophobic agenda. It is an interesting historical fact, however, that in the Muslim past these traditions were never taken as seriously as today, even by dedicated scholars. Equally, those scholars who did accept them as authentic usually tried to contextualise them. The famous thirteenth-century Sunni scholar al-Nawawi, for example, remarked in his *Minhaj bi Sharh Sahih Muslim* that the Prophet's dislike of *mukhannathun* could only apply to those *mukhannathun* who used their feminine charms for legally questionable purposes such as illicit sex and sex work, not to those who were simply born a *mukhannath*. This point is often neglected by modern Muslim scholars, but the very same argument can be found in the Egyptian scholar Shaykh Muhammad al-Tantawi's *fatwa* legalising gender reassignment surgery in 1988.[7]

In general, many Muslim scholars throughout the history of Islam have stressed that *mukhannathun* were as much a part of the Muslim community as everybody else and should be respected as such. This attitude persisted even amongst some otherwise quite staunch and unforgiving scholars. Ibn 'Abd al-Wahhab (d. 1792), progenitor of the now notorious variant of Sunni Islam called Wahhabism, once passed a *fatwa* in which he disapproved of inviting *mukhannathun* to festivities for entertainment but nevertheless stressed that *mukhannathun* should not be ostracised by Muslim communities and should instead be invited as guests to such festivities.

In the mystical literature of Islam, we find some stories which depict the *mukhannath* as a representative of the uncannily ambiguous and androgynous and therefore somehow related to the world of the spirit beings known as *jinn*, intelligent beings that can be good or bad, just as human beings. The famed Andalusian scholar and mystic Ibn 'Arabi (d. 1240) wrote in Chapter 9 of his *Futuhat*:

> People say that He [God] did not separate the first of the *jinns* as a female, as happened with Eve who was separated from Adam.

Some say that God created an opening within the body of the first
jinn, and part of it wedded the other part, and they had offspring
like the progeny of Adam, males and females who also wed each
other. *Jinns* were thus created hermaphrodite. This is why they
belong to the world of the *barzakh*: they share the natures of men
and of angels, in the same way as hermaphrodites share what is
male and what is female.[8]

In some parts of the Muslim world, there once existed a folk
belief according to which *mukhannathun* were the product of
mixed *jinn*-human sexual unions. The Devil himself is a *jinn* as
well, according to the scriptures of Islam, and is therefore sometimes depicted as a *khuntha* or *mukhannath*, an idea that has been
used to support transphobic, interphobic or homophobic ideas.
Ibn 'Arabi notes elsewhere in his *Futuhat*, however, that not only
jinn but also human souls can be of a hermaphroditic character.
This idea was elaborated on by many intellectuals in the Ottoman
Empire, Iran and South Asia, following in the footsteps of Ibn
'Arabi. As late as 1969, the Iranian spiritual master Ostad Elahi
wrote in his *Ma'rifat ar-Ruh*:

> All of the creatures endowed with a spirit on the planet Earth, in
> accordance with the Wisdom of nature and with their essential cre-
> ated disposition, fall into three groups: the first and second groups
> are those who are truly either male or female, who remain as they
> are in every bodily form and matter. The third group is the androgy-
> nous category, who by their original essential nature possess the
> aptitude and potentiality that fall between the other two groups.
> That is, they can become entirely male or female, as a result of
> particular changes or accidental causes; or they may remain in this
> androgynous condition. As can be seen in some cases, the sexual
> identities of some people do change after a certain period.[9]

Elahi based these musings on the teachings of the seventeenth-
century Iranian philosopher Mulla Sadra, who in turn was strongly
influenced by Ibn 'Arabi. Both Ibn 'Arabi and Mulla Sadra were

also seen as highly respected thinkers at the Mughal court and they have had a lasting influence on the spiritual life of Muslim South Asia. In fact, very similar ideas to the one quoted here from Elahi were, in Mughal-period Quranic commentaries, sometimes related to Verse 42:50 of the Quran: 'Or He combines the male and the female, and He renders whom he wills infertile. Indeed, He is knowledgeable and capable of creating anything.' The implication here, according to these commentators, is that the combination of male and female takes place in one single human being and that 'infertility' can also be interpreted as a general ineffectuality as far as heterosexual procreation is concerned.

There are also many traditions passed on in Islamic literature that caution the good Muslim against intolerance towards the *mukhannathun* because they may actually turn out to be especially blessed by God. In the *Risala* of the eleventh-century Muslim scholar al-Qushayri, an earlier Muslim scholar, 'Abd al-Wahhab al-Thaqafi, is quoted as saying:

> I once saw that a coffin was being carried by three men and a woman. I took the place of the woman, and we walked out to the cemetery, performed the prayers over the deceased, and buried him. Then I said to the woman, 'What relation was he to you?' The woman replied, 'He was my son.' I asked: 'Didn't you have some neighbours who could have helped you in this?' She answered: 'Yes, but they despised him.' Again, I asked: 'Why? What was he like then?' She replied: 'He was a mukhannath and the people despised him for that.' Then I felt sorry for her and took her in my house and gave her money, grain and clothing. That same night I saw an apparition, as if a moon-like person came to me wearing white clothes on the night of the full moon, and thanked me. 'Who are you?' I asked him. He replied: 'I am the mukhannath whom you buried today. God took pity on me because the people despised me.'

In another poignant story told by the thirteenth-century mystic Fariduddin 'Attar in his *Ilahinama*, a *mukhannath* proves to be the one who expresses true piety. In that story, a *mukhannath*, a Muslim scholar and a descendant of the family of the Prophet are taken captive by an infidel ruler. The infidel tells them to abjure Islam, otherwise he will execute the captives. The scholar thinks that he has the right to save his own life because God will forgive him the sin of abjuring Islam for his decades of scholarly service to the religion. The descendant of the family of the Prophet thinks that his ancestry will guarantee him a house in paradise anyway. Only the *mukhannath* thinks that he has nothing to lose in this world and, showing no arrogance, willingly becomes a brave martyr for Islam.

This same genre of Islamic literature often treated gender as more of a dynamic relationship than a matter of biology implying destiny. In another of his works, Fariduddin 'Attar remarked: 'When on the Day of Judgement God will call out "Oh Men!", the Virgin Mary will be the first to stand up.' Presenting a similar perspective, the thirteenth-century Indian sufi saint Jamal ud-Din Hansvi once wrote, 'Every seeker of the world is female, every seeker of the hereafter is a mukhannath, and every seeker of the Lord is male.' We find in these last two quotes a certain patriarchal attitude that identifies masculinity with true courageousness and spirituality, but it is, nevertheless, interesting that, to these sufi writers, these issues are neither tied to the biological sex nor the gender identity of a person. 'Attar emphasises in a related context elsewhere that the Prophet Muhammad (p.b.u.h.) had said, 'God does not look at your forms, He only looks at your inner constitution.' To other mystics, such as the North Indian saint Nizamuddin Auliya (d. 1325), gender seemed almost entirely irrelevant on the spiritual path. When questioned as to why he had such great respect for a female mystic called Fatima Sam, Nizamuddin Auliya reportedly replied: 'When a lion suddenly emerges out of the jungles, nobody ever asks whether it is a male or a female lion.'

In the discourses of Muslim law, however, there was often not as much freedom and dynamism as in mystical literature. The Muslim doctors of canonical law were, for example, very much troubled by the category of the intersex *khuntha*. As is commonly known, Islamic canonical law had at times developed quite distinct rules for men and women. Ever since the early Muslims had inherited scientific and medical wisdom from Byzantium, ancient Persia and India, Muslim scholars—who were often also medical professionals—had been aware that some bodies could not be easily classified as either male or female. What rules should be enforced for the *khuntha*? Should a *khuntha* inherit like a man or like a woman? Should a *khuntha* pray like a man or like a woman? We saw earlier such concerns expressed in the reply of scholar Adil Salahi to the *Arab News* journalist.

Muslim scholars were intent on finding out ways by which the 'dominant sex' of a *khuntha* could be determined. When speaking of a dominant sex here, it has to be understood that these scholars of jurisprudence were not interested in personal gender identity, but merely concerned with producing a legal definition of a 'physiological true sex' from which practical rules of everyday life could be derived. According to some traditions, the son-in-law of the Prophet, 'Ali ibn Abi Talib, had once suggested that one should pay attention to the way in which a *khuntha* urinates. Several later scholars have adopted this measure as well, at least in theory. Some have only derived from it even more complicated and convoluted considerations. Saqer A. Almarri notes:

> [The tenth-century scholar Al-Qadi al-Nu'man writes that] if the person has genital structures associated with both males and females, then a further examination is required to test which orifice urine is excreted from. If the urine is ejected through an orifice in the penis, then the person is deemed a male, whereas the person is deemed a female when urine is ejected through an orifice in the vulva. The situation becomes further complicated if the urine is excreted from

two orifices, a penile orifice and a vulvar orifice. If the urine is excreted from both orifices, the penile and the vulvar orifices, then the sex is determined according to the location of the first trickle of urine. This contrasts with the protocol of another Shi'i jurist AbuJa'far Al-Tusi's rule who establishes the last trickle as the criterion for the decision on the body's sex.[10]

In the discourses of Muslim scholars of canonical jurisprudence, we often notice a rather narrow obsession with the smallest details of a real or imagined intersex body that leaves little personal freedom for the individual concerned. Conversely, we also know of examples from Muslim history of scholars who were able to use the ambiguities of intersex bodies in the favour of those concerned. Khaled El-Rouayheb relates an interesting story, told by the Damascene judge Muhammad Akmal al-Din (d. 1603), of a man called 'Abd al-Rahman and a young bookbinder named 'Ali who had fallen in love with each other in the mid-sixteenth century. 'Ali was eventually discovered to be a *khuntha*, although raised as a boy. With the approval of a physician and the orders of the judge, 'Ali was officially declared female and was henceforth known as 'Aliyya. The bookbinder and her beloved 'Abd al-Rahman were now able to legally marry.[11] Here we may feel tempted to add: and they lived happily ever after. Not all such stories ended happily, however. Sara Scalenghe, who also recounts the story of 'Abd al-Rahman and 'Aliyya, details the case of a pious man who was deeply in love with a *khuntha* and had married her, considering her his wife. Out of jealousy, a rejected suitor of the *khuntha* brought the story to the attention of the respective city's ruler who, after medical examination, judged the wife to not be sufficiently female enough, annulled the marriage and publicly punished the couple.[12]

The modern phenomenon of people seeking gender reassignment surgery has posed similar questions for contemporary

Muslim scholars as the existence of castrated eunuchs and inter-sex people did for their precursors. I have already mentioned the 1988 *fatwa* by the Egyptian Sunni scholar Shaykh Muhammad al-Tantawi. Tantawi seemed not to have been too sure about the differences between a *khuntha*, a *mukhannath* and a transgender woman but, in any case, his *fatwa* allowed gender reassignment surgery for at least one transgender woman known as Sally. Tantawi's *fatwa* still remains contested in Egypt and is a pretty singular case in the Sunni world, but Shi'a Muslim scholars in particular have shown an openness towards gender reassignment. Several Shi'a scholars from Lebanon and Iran have permitted gender reassignment for transgender people. The most well-known example in that regard is the now somewhat infamous case of Ayatollah Khomeini, leader of the 1979 Islamic Revolution in Iran, passing a *fatwa* which accepted transsexuality as a perfectly natural condition and a part of God's creation and which also allowed transgender people to seek gender reassignment surgery. It is often said that Khomeini published this *fatwa* thanks to the insistence of the transgender activist Maryam Khatoon Molkara (d. 2012) who had already approached the Ayatollah many years before the Islamic Revolution. Thanks to Ayatollah Khomeini's *fatwa*, gender reassignment is legal in Iran today and is even supported financially by the state.

It is often claimed, however, that gender reassignment surgery in Iran functions as a double-edged sword; for transgender people it offers a pathway towards social acceptance and relief but it is simultaneously used to pressure homosexual men and women into relationships which conform to heterosexual gender binaries, while homosexual relationships remain strongly crimi-nalised. Sensationalist Western news outlets have from time to time claimed that the Iranian government regularly forces gay men to 'undergo a sex change'. Afsaneh Najmabadi, however, the only scholar who has engaged in comprehensive research on the subject thus far, notes that the picture is not quite so black and white.[13] While, according to her, homosexual and transgender Iranians endure a lot of social pressure, some of it supported by the government, in actuality not even transgender people are forced to undergo gender reassignment. Although a *fatwa* in Khomeini's *Tahrir al-Wasilah* suggested surgery as an option, at the same time it clarified that it is not obligatory (*wajib*) for transgender people.

Just like transgender people in many other societies, many Iranian transgender people choose to live their gender identity without undergoing any surgery at all and there are legal loopholes that make this possible in many cases. In fact, the above-mentioned activist Maryam Khatoon Molkara had already been granted a new birth certificate as a woman ten years before she was even able to go through gender reassignment surgery. The same legal loopholes also allow many people who identify as queer or non-binary to find new ways of expressing their gender and their sexuality without having to fear negative legal consequences. To carve out a life within such loopholes requires resilience and creativity. It is not possible for everybody and may be experienced as very difficult by some. But for many others, Najmabadi notes, it has allowed for the emergence of a far wider practical diversity of sexualities and genders in post-revolutionary Iran than many people would believe.

Not all Muslim majority societies have accepted gender reassignment as readily as Iran, however. Malaysia offers a particularly saddening example of a multireligious society with a narrow Muslim majority where the rights of Muslim transgender people have been curbed over the course of the last few decades. Up until the 1980s, gender reassignment surgeries were regularly performed in Malaysia and most Muslim scholars found no reason to comment on this in any way. Since then, however, Malaysian Muslim scholars have become increasingly hostile in their opinions towards trans people in general and gender reassignment in particular.

In the years leading up to 2020, prominent Malaysian trans activists such as Nisha Ayub and the SEED Foundation, founded and run by the trans community in Malaysia, have been leading a brave fight against these hostile opinions, often with the equally brave support of the feminist collective Sisters in Islam. The current situation in Malaysia is especially painful, since the Malay Peninsula and Malay Muslim society has a long history of accepting trans people. In the past, the Malay *mak-nyah* was often seen as a 'third gender' that had been a very natural part of God's creation, similar to how *hijras* have been, and still are, seen by many South Asian Muslims. Comparable to the *khwajasara*, the *mak-nyah* also often held important positions at the courts of Malay sultans. Not much is left of these traditions today and LGBT people in general, transgender women in particular, are now often painted as representatives of a disruptive, decadent Western influence on Muslim societies.

Within just the four decades of my own lifetime, similar developments have taken place in many parts of the Muslim world. Traditional cultural niches for transgender and intersex people and even, to some extent, for homosexual desires could once be found in a lot of Muslim societies. Nowadays not many of these are given space to exist. The *mukhannathun*, in one form or another, were still somewhat socially visible without being persecuted in many Arab societies up until the nineteenth century. The last remnant of this could be found in the *khanith* of Oman—*khanith* being a derivative and portmanteau of *khuntha* and *mukhannath*—who were sometimes described by researchers and other visitors to the country in the 1970s as transgender and sometimes as feminine homosexual males. It was noted that the *khanith* were relatively accepted in society, often respected as entertainers and appeared as an integral part of women's parties.

This relative social acceptance seems to have disappeared almost completely now; '*khanith*' is mostly used as an insult today and stricter laws against 'cross-dressing' and homosexuality have been implemented. I have been told by friends in Oman that many straight Omani men still often seek out 'feminine males' for sexual favours in secret and that sexual harassment of them is very common. The Muslim scholar Ali Ghandour once told me that during his childhood in Morocco, transgender entertainers were still a very regular part of all important festivities. However, in recent decades public attitudes towards both transgender people and homosexuality have taken a turn for the worse and, as witnessed in a scandalous social media case in early 2020, transgender women and gay men sometimes publicly denounce each other in order to gain favour in the eyes of the public.

Sometimes attitudes in Arabic-speaking Muslim societies can be a complicated mix of the traditional and the modern. A Tunisian friend who identifies both as gay and non-binary trans had to flee his country because of serious threats of homophobic violence from his own brother. Tunisia still criminalises homosexual acts and 'cross-dressing'. This friend also told me that many segments of Tunisian society are still relatively tolerant of feminine gay men and transgender women, as long as they are not associated too closely with their own family, mentioning that his own father was once actually quite fond of genderqueer artists. In almost all Arabic-speaking Muslim societies, however, attitudes have become significantly worse across the twentieth and early twenty-first century. A few remarkable court rulings in favour of LGBTQI rights have been pronounced recently in Lebanon, though these should be read against a wider context of discrimination and marginalisation faced by LGBTQI people in Lebanon.

The same trends can be detected in many other Muslim societies. Up until the 1990s, the *yan daoudou* of West African Hausa culture who, like the Omani *khanith*, are sometimes described as transgender, sometimes as feminine male homosexuals, have still been a relatively well-accepted part of Hausa society. In fact, like Indian *hijras*, *yan daoudou* had once been known as especially fervent Hajj pilgrims. Ever since the 1990s, however, they have experienced more and more brutal waves of persecution, both by revivalist Muslim movements and by evangelical Christian elements in the government of nations such as Nigeria. Many *yan daoudou* have tried to seek asylum in Europe, often adopting gay or transgender identities here. I have also been told by several Somali friends and acquaintances that in previous generations transfeminine people, sometimes called *khanith* as in Oman, had been an accepted part of society. A Somali trans friend once told me that her own grandmother had still believed that trans people were the work of the angels, while she faced much more discrimination from Somalis of her own and her parents' generation. Equally, while Turkey has a rich history of sexual diversity in the Ottoman period and one of its most celebrated singers, Bülent Ersoy, is a transgender woman, ordinary transgender people, just as gay men, lesbian women and other sexual minorities, have faced increasing repression under the Erdogan regime.

A memory of a different time is sometimes kept alive in the works of artists and intellectuals of Muslim majority countries. Saudi Arabian novelist Raja'a Alem made an androgynous person the hero of her *Khatam*, which is set in an early twentieth-century traditional Makkah long lost today. Throughout the novel the protagonist travels between male and female social spaces and we are never explicitly told whether they are a boy, girl, intersex person, or some other combination of male and female. Turkish author Elif Shafak, in *Pinhan*, told the story of an intersex person on a sufi journey in Ottoman times. These respective works offer a counterweight to reductive stories of Islamic history and culture and to narratives about Islam's conservative relationship to gender believed by many Muslims and non-Muslims in their respective societies today. A wide range of courageous queer artists engage in the same efforts today, despite facing social ostracism and political persecution for their efforts.

Compared to worrying developments in much of the Muslim world, the fact that South Asian Muslim transgender women, *hijras* and *khwajasaras* have been able to create activist spaces, gain public visibility and even achieve legal recognition both in Pakistan and India seems almost like a miracle. I believe that this 'miracle' owes much to the unique strength, mutual support and social organisation that the structures of traditional *gharanas* and *deras* offer to the South Asian community. Although many teachings of the older gurus are now disregarded by younger generations of activists, their resilience and confidence continues to live on in their spiritual children.

5

ON THE PATH OF THE SAINTS

IN 2016, I VISITED Delhi after a long time away. On this occasion, I was not staying with or visiting the *hijra* community. There had been a few rivalries between different *hijra* houses that had turned violent and I did not want to get involved, preferring to explore the city as a 'tourist'. This was a strange and unknown experience for me. Delhi seen through these eyes is a very different city than when viewed from a *hijra dera*. My friend Sambhav, a prominent queer activist, and his mother housed me in their atmospheric home in the middle of Old Delhi. Here, the rhythm of traditional life felt very similar to that which I had experienced in the *hijra* community. However, now I had much more freedom as far as my own movement was concerned and could explore the city according to my own whims.

My most beloved destinations in South Asia have always been the shrines of the Muslim saints. So I ventured out on a few tours to explore these sacred sites. Together with Sambhav, I visited the beautiful little shrine of Sarmad Kashani near the Jama Masjid. The seventeenth-century saint had been executed on the orders of the Mughal emperor Aurangzeb for scandalising the orthodox with both his lifestyle and his preaching. As far as his preaching is concerned, it must be noted that he was born a Jew in Iranian Kashan and, after converting to Islam, had become a wandering dervish, preaching a vision of unity that transcended all formal religions. As far as his lifestyle was concerned, what particularly troubled the public was that the naked mendicant was very vocal in his homoerotic love for a young Hindu man called Abhay Chand. Sarmad's execution may not have been induced by either of these peculiar issues but rather by the fact that he had become a confidant of Dara Shikoh, Aurangzeb's mystically minded brother and rival to the throne.

I recalled that during my earlier stays in Delhi I had passed the shrine of this saint a couple of times without ever actually visiting it. The area around the Jama Masjid was considered the traditional territory of another esteemed *hijra* line so we were careful not to show too much presence there. We usually only passed by during quick shopping trips to the bazaars. I had once bought DVDs of the movies *Pakeezah*, *Umrao Jaan* and *Heer Ranjha* there. Now, in the company of Sambhav, I was able to quietly pray my Fatiha for the saint and spread rose petals on his grave.

On one of the days after this, I went to the *dargah* (shrine) of Hazrat Nizamuddin Auliya q.s., one of the most esteemed sufi saints of India. This site has become quite popular with Western seekers of Indian spirituality ever since one of the teachers of Nizamuddin Auliya's line of the Chishti sufi order, Hazrat Inayat Khan (d. 1927), emigrated to the West, married an American called Ora Ray Baker—a relative of Christian Science Founder Mary Baker Eddy—and started to preach sufi mysticism in Europe. His daughter, Noor Inayat Khan, was to become a British spy who would fight the Nazis in World War II. She was eventually caught by the Germans and died in the Dachau concentration camp in 1944.

Noor's brother, Vilayat Inayat Khan (d. 2004), continued the sufi leadership of his father and it was him in particular who popularised visits to the Nizamuddin *dargah* in the hippie age. Up to this day, many Westerners come to listen to the sessions of Qawwali which take place there each Thursday evening. It also attracts many Indian visitors, who come not only to listen to the Qawwali but also to watch the flock of white people attempting to dress like Indian *sadhus*. On most other days, however, the shrine complex remains a fairly traditional example of Muslim shrine culture in Northern India. Other sufi saints are buried alongside Hazrat Nizamuddin, most importantly, Hazrat Ameer Khusrau q.s., Nizamuddin's companion, about whom I have more to say later.

My favourite place in the shrine complex is the grave of a woman: Princess Jahanara, sister of the aforementioned Dara Shikoh and a prolific writer on spiritual topics. Devotees, many of them also Hindu, come to pay their respect to the saints buried here, to pray, make wishes and to meditate. The pilgrims bring round baskets heavy with rose petals and embroidered *chadars* (sheets) to spread on the graves of the saints. Both can be purchased in the shops that shrewd businessmen have set up all around the shrine, but those who ignore their calls are able to obtain them for a much fairer price from one of the *khadims* (caretakers) at the entrance of the shrine. Pilgrims also tie little ribbons to the perforated stone screens surrounding the graves of the saints, symbolising wishes made. The air is heavy with the fragrance of incense and the smell of oil lamps.

Not all parts of the shrine are accessible to women. Cisgender women, that is. This is a specific regulation only found in some sufi shrines of South Asia. Many shrines allow equal access for both men and women. In some, such as this *dargah*, an orthodox desire for purity has introduced this rule. I will have a bit more to say on this in Chapter 6, but here it suffices for me to say that in Nizamuddin women are usually not permitted to enter the inner sanctum of the shrine but have their own place to pray.

When I was about to give my offerings and do my prayers, the *khadim* who had handed me the *chadar* and the basket full of rose petals asked me if I was a guru. A little dumbstruck and not fully understanding what he was hinting at, I replied, 'No.' The *khadim* then sent me to the ladies' section and brought my offerings into the inner sanctum, spreading them on the graves of Nizamuddin Auliya and Ameer Khusrau while I watched him through the perforated screens. Only much later, when I had left the shrine, did I realise that he had been politely asking whether I was transgender. Had I replied with 'Yes', I would have been able to enter the inner sanctum.

Having left the *dargah*, I tried to find an autorickshaw ride back to Old Delhi. The chances of getting one for a reasonable price are very low in Nizamuddin, particularly when you are white. I finally went with a driver who charged me far more than the usual price. After starting to talk to me, however, he became quite surprised by my fluent Urdu. He said that in his twenty-five years as a driver he had never met a foreigner who spoke such nice Urdu. Whether this was true or not, he was visibly excited about it, and changed from calling me 'ma'am' to calling me 'daughter' and finally 'sister'. At every traffic light he turned around to ask me questions, missing the light changes on a couple of occasions. He also dropped the price of the rickshaw ride considerably but, given that he was such lovely company, I decided to pay him the fare we had originally agreed.

When we finally reached our destination in Old Delhi, the rain was pouring down heavily. The driver, whose name was Qayyum Khan, insisted that I wait in his rickshaw until the rain stopped. He implored me to take my money back a few times but I declined. It continued to rain for at least half an hour. So, we sat there in his autorickshaw and talked. About Germany, about India, about life, about Muslims in India. He told me about his village in Uttar Pradesh, about his family and his children. A few moments of this conversation remain fondly in my memory. He asked me with whom I was staying in Old Delhi and I replied 'with a friend'. He asked if the friend was Muslim. Half-jokingly, I responded, 'Unfortunately not.' He replied that this was not an unfortunate thing as 'Faith is a matter of the heart. And it is God's will that there are Muslims and non-Muslims.' Then he quoted a poetic verse to the effect that the moon would be nothing without the stars and that a lover is nothing without competition. He also said that Delhi is the *'awliya ki chokhat'* (threshold of the saints), the actual Holy Land of Islam. And that, therefore, all of my prayers here would be answered.

He treated me with a kind of respect that I had rarely seen in life. Part of this respect stemmed from me being a transgender person. He didn't notice immediately. But he asked me why, at the age of thirty-six, I was not married and had no children. For Qayyum Khan, the existence of transgender people was as much a God-given reality as the existence of different religious communities. And it was just right that all this diversity in God's plan would come together at the threshold of the saints.

That day in Nizamuddin recalled for me some of the first interactions I'd had with people at Indian sufi shrines back when I first met with the *hijra* community sixteen years before. The first trip that Annie and I undertook together was from Mumbai to Ajmer in Rajasthan. Ajmer, usually referred to by Muslims as Ajmer Shareef (Noble or Holy Ajmer), is the holiest place of Islam in India. The saint Khwaja Ghareeb Nawaz Moinuddin Chishti, founder of the South Asian Chishti sufi order to which Nizamuddin Auliya of Delhi also belonged, lies buried here and a grand shrine has been built around his grave. Unlike the shrine of Nizamuddin Auliya in Delhi, women and men are not usually separated here. At least, that was the case when I visited. Annie and I were there for the *urs*, the yearly festival of the saint that is always celebrated at such shrines across South Asia. The *urs* of Ajmer is the biggest in India, drawing pilgrims from all over the subcontinent. Even Pakistani politicians have given their obeisances to the saint on this occasion. Benazir Bhutto, for example, visited the *dargah* of Ajmer several times during her political career.

In Ajmer, we were guests in the house of one of the *khadims*. Just as in Nizamuddin so many years later, the old pious *khadim* with his long white beard treated us with the utmost respect. Fresh from the environment of my mosque back in Germany, this experience impressed me immensely. Why did this old pious Muslim man give so much respect to this queer practically-still-a-teenager? At some point I asked him very directly what he thought of 'people like me'. He said that the saints have always respected us and considered us their peers.

In fact, there has always been a close connection between the shrines of Muslim saints in South Asia and the *hijra* and *khwa-jasara* communities. When journalists or researchers ask me for contacts to the *hijra* community, I am reluctant to hand them out because I have seen that far too often they are not handled responsibly. Instead I tell journalists and researchers that the easiest way to find *hijras* or *khwajasaras* in South Asia is to visit an *urs* of one of the Muslim saints. You can always find the community gathering there.

The word *urs* itself has a connotation that can almost be described as transgender. The word is of Arabic origin and in that language it refers to a marriage or a wedding. What is indicated is the 'wedding' of the saint with his eternal Beloved: God Himself. The *urs* usually takes place on the anniversary of the death of the saint which the followers of traditional Islam envision as a mystical nuptial night. God in Islam is always seen as a being without any gender, of course, but in the language of the poets this wedding night is often described using very gendered words. In some forms of mystical Muslim poetry God is imagined like a beloved woman, often symbolised by the mythical Leyla (or Laila) of the romantic Leyla and Majnun epic. But far more often, especially in South Asia, the mystic is imagined as a bride waiting for her bridegroom. This idea crosses religious lines, for the Hindu saint Tulsi Das is often quoted as having said that in the context of devotion only God is male while all devotees are female.

In the world of that imagery, being transgender could actually be described as the norm and not the exception. And, in fact, many of the Muslim saints of South Asia have been known to cross gendered lines in their lives. The Punjabi poet saint Bulleh Shah, whose shrine can be found in the Pakistani city of Qasur today, was known to have spent his days in the company of sex workers and *hijras* and scandalised the public by dancing with ankle bells on, like a courtesan. His poetry contains abundant examples of the saint imagining himself as a female lover adoring either God or his spiritual master as a male beloved.

A particularly popular story with a similar sentiment is told about Nizamuddin Auliya and his companion Ameer Khusrau. Ameer Khusrau, who contributed much to the development of classical Indian music and is especially known as a poet today, was a devoted student of his spiritual master Nizamuddin. Numerous poems of Khusrau's, today often sung as Qawwalis, attest to the student's love for his master. One day, a nephew of Nizamuddin Auliya's passed away at a terribly young age and the saint was grief-stricken for a long time. Ameer Khusrau became very worried about his spiritual teacher and feared for his health. One day, he saw a group of women, all dressed in yellow, playing music on a *dholak* and bringing mustard flowers to a nearby temple. He asked someone what this was about and was informed that the women celebrated the spring festival, Basant. Hearing this, Ameer Khusrau put on the bracelets of a Hindu woman, dressed in yellow just like the women and went to Nizamuddin's doorstep while playing the *dholak*. When Hazrat Nizamuddin saw this he was delighted and smiled for the first time after many weeks. Nizamuddin celebrated the Basant festival every year since and it is celebrated until this day at his shrine.

Some of the *khadims* at the Nizamuddin *dargah* nowadays dispute that Ameer Khusrau was actually donning female dress on this occasion, in line with more conformist interpretations of

113

Islam. Another story demonstrates that such transgressions were already hotly debated in the thirteenth century, the period contemporary to Nizamuddin Auliya. Musa was another student of Nizamuddin Auliya who was of a much more staunch bent than Ameer Khusrau. He highly disapproved of the fact that his spiritual master was regularly visited by the courtesans and *hijras* of Delhi who often even sang and danced at Nizamuddin's *dargah*. One day, he was going on the Hajj pilgrimage and also planned to visit the grave of Prophet Muhammad (p.b.u.h.) in Madinah. A few miles before the gates of Madinah, though, he suddenly became very sick and was unable to proceed any further.

At night, Musa had a vision. He heard the voice of the Messenger of God: 'How can you visit me, while you prevent those who want to visit my beloved from coming to him?' Musa immediately understood what the vision was hinting at and repented. When he returned to India, not only did he ask the courtesans and *hijras* for forgiveness, he even started to live and dress like a *hijra* himself. Musa became known as 'Musa Shah-e Suhag', which can roughly be translated as 'Musa the Lord of Bridal Bliss'. Up to this day, his shrine in Gujarat is attended by dervishes who either live completely as *hijras* or wear some aspects of female-coded dress and jewellery. They are known as 'the suhagi dervishes' and, in their honour, I used to write under the pen name Leyla Suhagi when I first started to publish about the *hijra* community online.

The case of Musa Shah-e Suhag demonstrates that quite often the lines between *hijras* and sufi dervishes can be blurred and, in fact, in a lot of regions of Muslim South Asia *hijras* and *khwajasaras* are considered a type of dervish. In the Pakistani region of Sindh in particular *khwajasaras* are often referred to as *'faqeer'*, literally an Arabic word for a poor person but in the South Asian context usually used to denote wandering sufis. Indeed, many *hijras* do see themselves as a kind of sufi. The social structure of the *hijra* and *khwajasara* community, with its gurus, *chelas* and *deras*, is one that has been fashioned after the structure of religious orders and I have experienced several times at an *urs* of a saint that the dervishes and sufis present often viewed the *hijra* gurus and their *chelas* as their spiritual equivalents. Like dervishes, *khwajasaras* often refer to their own community as the community of the *Allahwale*, the 'people belonging to God', while the people of mainstream society are referred to as the *dunyawale*, 'the people belonging to the world'.

Traditionally, a specific religious significance was often given to those *hijras* in particular who had undergone a voluntary ritual castration. Such *hijras* were always referred to as *nirvan*, the modern Hindi/Urdu version of the better-known 'nirvana', expressing an ideal of asceticism and renunciation. Indeed, some Muslim dervishes without any connection to the *khwajasara* community had in the past sometimes chosen to undergo voluntary castration, even though castration was frowned upon by Islamic canonical law. The castration was meant to render the recipient free of worldly sexual desires and thus also closer to God, although it had the additional positive effect of a certain feminisation of the body. Many *khwajasaras* nowadays opt for more elaborate and advanced forms of gender reassignment surgery, if they can afford to do so. Ironically, these *khwajasaras* often still consider themselves *nirvan*.

In the past, some *khwajasaras* have become sufi saints themselves and shrines have been built around their remains. The grave of the Pakistani *khwajasara* saint Sohni Faqeer (lit. 'the beautiful *faqeer*') can be found in the city of Mirpur Khas in the province of Sindh. Sohni Faqeer was born before the Partition of India in 1947 to a Hindu Brahmin family. Originally, Sohni Faqeer and her family, like most Hindus of Mirpur Khas, had left for India after Partition. But, after a while, Sohni returned, perhaps because there had been a conflict with her family due to her gender identity. She converted to Islam and became an initiated member of the *khwajasara* community. It was then that the name Sohni was given to her, due to her extraordinary beauty. Sohni Faqeer became a very pious Muslim and eventually retreated to a local *imambargah*, a Shi'a Muslim shrine for the members of the household of Prophet Muhammad (p.b.u.h.). For many decades she took care of the *imambargah* and the nearby grave of a sufi saint and often blessed the visitors of these two holy places. She was well-known for her compassion and her great love for little children. After she passed away she was buried on the grounds of the *imambargah* and nowadays local women often visit her grave to pray for a desired pregnancy.

Imambargahs often play an important part in the spiritual culture of the community. Amongst the saints highly revered in traditional *khwajasara* and *hijra* culture are the Ahl ul-Bayt, the members of the household of the Prophet, in particular the Prophet's daughter Fatima (a.s.), her husband Imam 'Ali (a.s.) and their two sons Hassan and Hussayn (a.s.). While performing the Hajj pilgrimage was an essential step to becoming a respected guru in my *hijra* house in Delhi, no Hajj was considered fully complete without visits to the shrines of Imam 'Ali and Hussayn in Najaf and Karbala in Iraq. Claire Pamment has written about the importance of Shi'a imagery to *khwajasaras* in Pakistan, even within the framework of a modern transgender rights movement. The reverence for this holy family gives the Islam traditionally practised in a lot of *hijra* and *khwajasara* communities a decidedly Shi'ite flavour, even though only a few members of the community would explicitly identify themselves as Shi'a Muslims. In fact, when in the early 2000s I was asking Muslim *hijras* in Delhi whether they came from a Sunni or Shi'a background, most had no idea what they were, an attitude that was not uncommon amongst lower-income Indian Muslims of that time.

Sweeping contemporary political analyses often speak of an eternal clash of Sunni and Shi'a Islam, but it should be noted that traditionally a lot of what is called Sunni Islam in South Asia has often had a certain Shi'ite influence, frequently mediated by sufi saints who often claimed to be both spiritual and physical descendants of the Ahl ul-Bayt. Scholars such as Marshall Hodgson and Wilferd Madelung noted that, in fact, what was later called Sunni Islam and is now often seen as the mainstream tradition of Islam originally emerged out of a compromise between early Shi'ites and their opponents. In the history of Islam, this influence has sometimes been more and sometimes less visible.

In the early modern period, Islam in the region between the Balkans and Bengal was characterised by constantly overlapping Sunni and Shi'a spaces. In the Sunni Islam preached by Wahhabis and Salafis today, any influence of or even sympathy for Shi'a positions has become completely undetectable. In traditional South Asian Sunni Islam as it was still mostly practised just a few decades ago, the influence of Shi'a Islam has often been very strong. On the other hand, far away from the centres of Shi'ite political power in Iran and urban centres of Shi'a scholars such as Lucknow, many South Asian Shi'a Muslims have seen themselves more as a quiet spiritual elite within the greater fold of Muslims than representing a religious confession that can be clearly demarcated from other confessions.

This has created a very specific religious culture that has sometimes been described as a crypto-Shi'ite Sunnism. In Punjab in particular, there existed until not so long ago a tradition of people who, while outwardly belonging to the Sunni sufi order of the Qadiris and not identifying themselves as in any way having a different confession to their Sunni neighbours, clandestinely passed on specific Shi'a practices and beliefs within their family circles. This was especially common amongst Sayyids, who consider themselves direct descendants of the Ahl ul-Bayt. One of the most populous tribes of rural Punjab, the Awans, also claim descent from Imam 'Ali and while most Awans are quite staunch Sunnis, this imagined or real family relation has often made them receptive to Shi'i claims as well.

Non-conforming wandering dervishes like the Qalandars, Malangs and Madaris do not follow any formal Shi'a law but proudly declare themselves as followers of the Ahl ul-Bayt. Other prominent sufis of South Asia, such as the Sindhi saint Shah Abdul Lateef Bhitai or the Punjabi Awan saint Sultan Bahu, declared themselves to be beyond Sunni and Shi'a. A significant number of the population of the Punjab and Sindh tries to evade the question of confession altogether by simply describing themselves as 'Maulayi' (belonging to the Maula, i.e. Imam 'Ali) instead of using a charged word such as Shi'a.

For many decades this kind of fluid religiosity has also been a vital part of pop culture in the independent nations of Pakistan and India: Indian devotional movies like *Niyaz aur Namaaz* (1977), Bollywood hits like *Coolie* (1983) and Pakistani Punjabi blockbusters like *Aasoo Billa* (1971) have all expressed this kind of religiosity in several ways. When, in 1974, the Bangladeshi singer Runa Laila recorded a version of the sufi song *Dama Dam Mast Qalandar*, a song praising both the Sindhi Qalandar saint Laal Shahbaaz Qalandar and Imam 'Ali, for the Indian movie *Ek se badkar ek*, it became an instant hit across the subcontinent. When I was going out on *badhai* with the *hijra* groups in New Delhi in 2005, this song was still one of the most requested for us to sing and perform to, even in majority Sikh and Hindu areas. The song also remains one of the most popular ones to which Pakistani *khwajasaras* perform the *dhamaal*, an ecstatic sufi dance. The *dhamaal* is usually performed at sufi shrines but in *khwajasara* culture a *dhamaal* also often precedes all other dances at rather worldly festivities (such as 'birthday' balls), to express respect towards God and the saints before the party starts.

All these expressions of blurred lines between Sunni, Sufi and Shi'a Muslim identities have increasingly come under siege since the 1970s, in Pakistan in particular and even more so under the military dictatorship of Zia-ul-Haq, who dreamed of turning the country into an Islamic state following Saudi Arabian models. Since then, sectarian identities in South Asia have become much more politicised and blurred lines are much less tolerated. When the famed sufi singer Amjad Sabri was murdered by anonymous gunmen in 2016, it was often pointed out that one reason for his murder may have been that he repeatedly stood up for an inclusive Islam that is nourished by Shi'a elements as much as by Sunni Sufism. His murder was certainly a sign of the threatened status of such an Islam and has been a symptom of a development that has led to massive anti-Shi'a rallies and attacks on Muharram mourners by Sunni extremists in 2020. However, in some quarters of South Asian Muslim society, including many traditional *khwajasara* houses, this inclusive Islam still lives on.

In the imagery, myths and symbols surrounding the Ahl ul-Bayt, the people of the household are often envisioned as both oppressed and marginalised and, at the same time, the protectors of the oppressed and marginalised. This symbolism has been so strong and pervasive that it has not only inspired faithful Shi'a Muslims throughout the ages but even modern members of the Communist Party like the writer Ismat Chughtai and the poets Faiz Ahmed Faiz and Kaifi Azmi. Imam 'Ali, his wife and his descendants are envisioned by religious and atheist alike as the heroes of all who feel oppressed and disinherited. The family of the Prophet is often imagined as those whose rights were ignored by the larger *ummah* (Muslim community).

This ignorance had its tragic climax in the event of Karbala in 680, when the grandson of the Prophet, Husayn, and his relatives and followers were massacred by the troops of the Umayyad caliph Yazeed. Mourning for this tragedy in the month of Muharram has traditionally been a practice not only strictly observed by Shi'a Muslims but also by Sunnis and even many

Hindus in South Asia. In other parts of the Islamic world, such as Morocco, the day on which Husayn was killed was turned into a celebration (here, of course, not identified with the story of the grandson of the Prophet). In more recent years, many Muslims worldwide have started to celebrate the beginning of Muharram as a New Year festival. In South Asia this traditionally used to be unthinkable: across religious lines it was agreed upon by every-body that the whole month of Muharram should be a month of mourning. Courtesans and other entertainers and sex workers would customarily close their businesses for the duration of the month. *Khwajasaras* have always joined the mourning processions with special fervour. In India I have also known many *hijras* who would stop wearing make-up during Muharram, even when going out on *badhai*.

My experience of these sentiments and the practice of symbols around the Ahl ul-Bayt has fundamentally changed my own out-look on Islam and its history as well. The mosque that I went to as a teenager in Germany had some vestiges of a traditional Turkish Sunni culture tied to Sufism and love for the Ahl ul-Bayt as well. But it also had a clear bent towards a modern Salafi-tinged Sunni Islam. I grew up with the idea that all the compan-ions of the Prophet had been faultless, that the history of early Islam had been perfect and that God had made sure that the consensus of the dominant Muslim scholars would always be right. However, the fervent love for the Ahl ul-Bayt and the mourning for their disinheritance and disenfranchisement that I encountered in South Asia told me something else. I now believe that the true Islam is found in the small voices, the oppressed voices and the disenfranchised voices. It is with the marginalised of history, not with the victorious. That, to me, also includes the many queer voices in Islam that have been erased from history.

Doctrinal Shi'a Islam in South Asia and elsewhere is today often characterised by a very strict adherence to the particularities of religious law. Shi'a Islam is, in its dominant manifestation, today characterised by a hierarchy of traditional scholars of the so-called Usuli school (from the Arabic word for 'principles') centred around Iraq and Iran. These Usuli scholars, whom we in the West often call 'the Ayatollahs', have created an ambitious mix of democracy and theocracy in present day Iran that we have learned to regard as the epitome of religious conservativism and social repression. But, as J.R.I. Cole mentions, for much of the nineteenth century, the Usuli scholars had minimal influence on most Shi'a Muslims of South Asia.[1] Artisans and working-class Shi'a Muslims in particular often considered the scholars lackeys of the rich, with no real religious authority. Instead, their Shi'a religiosity was much more centred around a fervent love for the Ahl ul-Bayt and it was often characterised by a leniency and clemency that was motivated by an almost secularist philosophy.

Before the Islamic Revolution in Iran, most Shi'a Muslims in South Asia (and elsewhere) held the position that before the coming advent of the last Imam at the end of time, no human being has the right to speak or legislate in the name of God. A much-beloved anecdote, often told in those circles but attested to from the earliest days of Islam, is the story of a female sex worker who was brought before Imam 'Ali to be executed for adultery. Imam 'Ali asked the woman why she did this work that was not considered appropriate in Islamic law. The woman explained to him that she was a poor widow who had to feed several children and that circumstances had forced her to take up this work. Imam 'Ali set the woman free and told the people not to punish her. Rather, he said, those people should be punished who created a world in which a poor widow had to struggle so much. In some other anecdotes it is said that one of the later descendants of 'Ali, Imam Ja'far, often tolerated it when some of his weaker companions drank alcohol from time to time, merely admonishing them every now and then and praying for forgiveness for them.

This kind of Shi'a Islam has, for very understandable reasons, become very popular with the socially marginalised. Courtesans and sex workers in particular have often identified strongly with it. In many cities of Northern India and Pakistan, it is often traditional red light districts such as Lahore's Heera Mandi which have become sites for the most fervent expressions of Shi'i faith. From the times of the royal palaces of the Mughal Empire on, *khwajasara* culture has often been in close contact with courtesan culture and many *khwajasaras* live in districts such as Heera Mandi. It is therefore no surprise that the *khwajasara* community would develop similar sentiments about Shi'i faith. We have already seen that, in modern times, prominent Shi'a scholars have often been much more open towards accepting transgender people as a natural part of God's creation and towards supporting gender reassignment, which is also appreciated by many South Asian *khwajasaras*.

Additionally, it has to be understood that historically it was often the princely states and kingdoms of India with the strongest Shi'a influence that were most formative in the development of both courtesan and *khwajasara* culture. Here, in particular, the Deccan Sultanates and their successor state Hyderabad should be mentioned, as well as the Kingdom of Awadh in what is today the Indian state of Uttar Pradesh. In both regions we find many fascinating examples of courtly *khwajasaras* patronising Shi'a piety by funding *imambargahs*, Muharram processions, ceremonies in honour of the members of the Ahl ul-Bayt and poets to write elegies for the Ahl ul-Bayt.

In Chapter 3, I mentioned Almas Ali Khan, the most powerful court eunuch in the kingdom of Awadh/Lucknow from the end of the eighteenth to the beginning of the nineteenth century. Almas was born into a poor family which sold the unusual child to the court in Lucknow. He entered into the service of the Lucknow court and quickly earned the love and trust of the ruler

Nawab Asaf ud-Daula and his mother Bahu Begum. Almas (diamond) was the name given to him by the eunuch society at court, royal eunuchs often being named after jewels and precious stones (we do not know of his name prior to this).

Almas eventually became the second most powerful person in the Kingdom of Awadh. He possessed land that made up more than a third of Awadh, had his own military force that was actually larger than the army of the *nawab* and managed extensive commercial operations. He also invested extensively in several projects for the development of Awadh and patronised artists and poets. More than anything else, however, he patronised the establishment of sacred enclosures and ceremonies for the remembrance of the martyrdom of Imam Husayn. He sponsored numerous Muharram processions and gatherings in memory of the Imam throughout his life and erected a large number of *imambargahs* and mosques throughout Awadh. Up to this day, some of the most revered holy places of Shi'a Islam in Lucknow and other cities in Uttar Pradesh owe their existence to Almas Ali Khan's charitable work.

Hyderabad owes one of its most noticeable religious landmarks to a courtly *khwajasara* as well. During the times of the Qutb Shahi dynasty there lived a *khwajasara* who was employed as a senior eunuch at the royal court. Like Almas Ali Khan, this *khwajasara* was also named after a precious stone. His name was Yaqut and he was known as especially pious and god fearing. In the year 1578, Yaqut got very ill, with few hopes of recovering. But one night he had a dream: someone told him that Imam 'Ali was calling him and led him to a hill in the vicinity of Hyderabad. There, on that hill, Imam 'Ali stood surrounded by light. In the dream, 'Ali rested his hand on one of the rocks of the hill. When Yaqut woke up his illness was gone and he felt strong and healthy again. He went out to the hill that he had seen in his dream. And there he also found a rock with the strange imprint of a hand.

Yaqut told his story at the court. People started to flock to the hill to see the holy imprint of Imam 'Ali's hand. After a while, the hill was named 'Maula Ali' (Lord Ali). A shrine was built on the orders of the Qutb Shahi Sultan. It turned into a famous place of pilgrimage and a festival began that each year, starting from Imam 'Ali's birthday on the thirteenth of Rajab until the seventeenth of Rajab, would be held on the hill. It was not only visited by the Shi'a Muslims of the area but by Sunnis and Hindus alike and remained important for harmonious interfaith relations in the Hyderabad area for many centuries. The shrine and the festival was subsequently not only patronised by the *khwajasaras* of the city but also by the courtesans and dancing girls. A number of famous courtesans devoted large sums of money to maintain the festival and especially to feed the poor on this occasion. Other courtesans donated guest houses for the pilgrims as well as pools, fountains and parks in the countryside nearby.

The most famous courtesan to patronise Maula Ali was Mah Laqa Bai Chanda, the famed female poet of the Deccan who may have been one of several real life inspirations for Mirza Hadi Rusva's celebrated Urdu novel *Umrao Jaan Ada* (1899), which was subsequently adapted as a Pakistani movie (1972); two Indian movies (1981; 2006); and a Pakistani drama series (2003). It was said that Mah Laqa Bai's birth in 1764 had been under the protection of Imam 'Ali and the shrine. During pregnancy her mother, also a courtesan, suffered from severe bleeding which almost led to a miscarriage. But she was miraculously healed after visiting the Maula Ali shrine. Throughout her life, Mah Laqa Bai Chanda remained one of the most dedicated devotees of the shrine. She and her mother were buried right next to the hill, in a mausoleum that was only recently renovated, thanks to the efforts of Scott Siraj al-Haqq Kugle, a queer Muslim scholar in the US, who has written extensively about Mah Laqa Bai and her poetry.[2]

Traditional *khwajasara* culture draws heavily on this rich historical heritage of Sufism, traditional Sunni Islam, Shi'a Islam and the legacy of courtesans and court eunuchs. As Pamment has pointed out, this heritage continues to be visible even in *khwajasara* spaces that are increasingly interacting with more globalised conceptions of what it means to be transgender. She notes that:

> Assertions of piety, drawing creatively from Sufi and Shi'a modes and performed by khwaja siras often on the fringes or on the lower rungs of developmental activism (viz. NGOs and CBOs), offer an embodied outlet for negotiating multiple axes of exclusion... These particular performances, drawing from Sufi and Shi'a modes, have negotiated spaces... to push against the dominant moral-religious and developmentalist rationalities that have tried to script legitimate khwaja sira identities in this era of rights.[3]

As such, this heritage continues to be an important pole around which *khwajasara* identities revolve and which assures them of a special place both in their local context and in the global sphere. As we shall see in Chapter 9, however, other visions of Islam have already started to encroach on this heritage and threaten to harm it significantly.

6

BEING A WOMAN

'*MAIN AURAT NAHIN HOON, main khusra hoon,*' I had said to the bearded gentleman who had tried to keep me from entering the shrine. 'I am not a woman, I am a *khusra.*' Here I employed a word for *khwajasara* that is now often considered politically incorrect in Pakistan and that could be translated as 'fag' or 'tranny'. In contrast to my encounter with the *khadim* at the shrine of Nizamuddin Auliya in Delhi, in this case I had entered the shrine fully aware of the fact that my 'transgender privilege'—perhaps one of the only contexts in which I could use this phrase—would give me access to the space of an inner sanctum that I would not be able to enter as a cisgender woman.

This was in 2017. I was part of the AKS Film Festival, founded by the Danish-Pakistani filmmaker Saadat Munir, and we were in Lahore. As part of a little outing, the artists and speakers who had been invited to this film festival, a mix of queer and trans people from Pakistan and the West, had visited the shrine of the sufi saint Shah Jamal. Shah Jamal had during his lifetime actually held a rather orthodox and staunch reputation; he was known for fighting against the religious syncretism that was preached at the Mughal court at that time. In our times, however, his shrine is widely rumoured to be a popular cruising ground for men seeking sexual encounters with other men. When we, as a group, entered the shrine and I was about to enter the inner sanctum, a bearded man, who had just left through the gate, angrily said to me, 'Ladies not allowed inside.' Hence came my reply, '*Main aurat nahin hoon, main khusra hoon.*' After that, I proceeded to enter and say my prayers there without any further hindrance.

Later I had to really think about what I had said there. My words had seemed very natural to me and appropriate within that specific setting. Indeed, when moving in India and Pakistan I am quite often very consciously adopting a *khwajasara/hijra* identity. In 2017, however, a strong debate in Western feminist discourse was raging between those who insisted on the inclusion of transgender women in their fight and certain cisgender feminists who insisted that transgender women are not truly women. (The latter are referred to as TERFs, trans exclusionary radical feminists, a term that is not a slur but merely descriptive.) With my own insistence on my specific transgender privilege at the shrine of Shah Jamal, was I not implicitly giving value to the argument upheld by TERFs? Was this not a contradiction in my own self-perception? In fact, if in the West anybody should claim I was not a woman, I would feel deeply offended. How was I able to employ my 'otherness' from women in Pakistan whilst in Europe I insisted on being a woman?

But here is the issue as it presents itself to me: being a woman is not a self-evident thing as such, even though both TERFs and many trans activists would claim that it is. This particular issue is precisely what the whole debate between inclusive feminists and TERFs revolves around. A comparable issue relating to the relationship between biology and gendered categorisation can also be seen at some sufi shrines in South Asia. It is a common misconception that women are banned from the inner sanctum of shrines in South Asia because of the seductive influence they may have on men. That is not the actual reason for their exclusion, however. First of all, not all shrines in South Asia maintain this separation of genders. There are several shrines, especially in the regions of Rajasthan and Sindh, where it is very common for women to enter the inner sanctum as well.

While it seems that more restrictive traditions have grown up in Punjab and the Delhi area, even here the issue is not one of sexual distraction. In fact, while *khwajasaras* usually go to the mosque or on Hajj in very androgynous plain white dress, when visiting a shrine they often dress up in glittery clothes—sometimes even quite revealing outfits—and full make-up. This can cause quite a few male gazes to be diverted. But that has never caused them to be barred from entry. I owe it to anthropologist Omar Kasmani to understand that the issue here is one of ritual purity. According to some expressions of a more legalist Islam, women are ritually impure while they menstruate as well as after childbirth. These interpretations have recently been challenged by feminist readings of Muslim scripture but they still remain ingrained in many Muslim societies and even more so in South Asia, where even stronger taboos about menstruating women exist in some Hindu communities as well.

These taboos are always related to a certain power that women possess during that time. In fact, the impure and the sacred are often very closely related in Muslim conceptions, as is demonstrated very well by the word *haram* which can relate as much to something forbidden (e.g. pork) as to something holy (e.g. the mosque in Makkah). Not rarely is it claimed in South Asia that menstruating women possess a certain mesmerism that can have a physical effect on their surroundings. Menstrual blood is, due to its inherent power, an indispensable ingredient in many procedures of black magic. It is this combination of impurity and mesmerism that, in some imaginations, should not clash with the presence of the saint, even in some cases where the saint is female herself. In some cases where there is gender segregation at sufi shrines, exceptions are not only made for *khwajasaras* but also for women who are visibly past the age of menstruation and childbirth as they are believed to be unable to cause danger anymore.

I have already indicated elsewhere that sometimes infertile women are seen as a type of *khwajasara* or *hijra* in South Asia as well. This seems to happen less and less frequently these days, probably owing to better medical knowledge about the causes of infertility and the realisation that it is often not the woman's fault if she is unable to get pregnant by her husband. But during my time in Delhi in the early 2000s, I still heard of cases in which some such women had been admitted to a *dera* and initiated into a *hijra gharana*. This demonstrates that *khwajasara/hijra* is a dynamic and fluid category that can indeed overlap with Western conceptions of what a cisgender woman is. It also shows that who may or may not be seen as a 'real woman' is always subject to cultural expectations.

Western feminists of previous generations, such as Simone de Beauvoir, have often noted that ideas that link being a 'real woman' to the status of her reproductive organs are intrinsically tied to patriarchal expectations. As such, feminism has been very crucial in developing an understanding of gender as socially constructed and culturally situated. The emergence of the TERF is a curious digression from this development, yet also a very telling symptom of how uncomfortable we feel with questioning assumptions held for generations.

The truth is, our binary understanding of gender and what makes a woman is neither more nor less murky than traditional South Asian understandings. In recent decades, we have become more and more aware of this murkiness, leading to a reactionary backlash around ideas of gender. We can also see this reactionary pattern in the phenomenon of the rise of the 'New Right' in many societies. The more we become aware of the complexities of our globalising world, of constant international interactions and cultural influences, of migration and hybridity, the more some people want to retreat to very simple and formulaic ideas about national and racial identity. Similarly, the more we become aware of sexual diversity, of the issues of transgender people and the existence of intersex people, the more some people feel threatened and insist even more fervently on the orthodoxy of their own identities. This is, of course, not just cisgender and heterosexual people; I have already mentioned about how some trans activists in the West feel very threatened by the idea of a third gender and are unwilling to accept that *khwajasaras* could have as clear an understanding of themselves as they do.

Awareness of the issues of intersex people poses a particular challenge to all binary conceptions of gender. The common understanding in our societies even today is that gender is based on a clearly defined binary biological sex that consists of coinciding chromosome sets (XY and XX) and genitalia (penis vs. vagina). Every divergence from the rule of this coincidence is seen as an aberration and essentially as a disease. Surgeries performed on the bodies of intersex babies to make them align with these understandings have long been compulsory in most Western societies. Even though legal realities have fortunately changed for the better in that regard, parents and doctors usually still opt for these surgeries today, even though surgeries and further medical treatments can cause intersex children a considerable amount of trauma and often have devastating consequences for them.

It is certainly the case that in most societies the majority of people fit into these binaries of sexuality and gender. There are exceptions—in one community in the Dominican Republic, for example, some children develop penises with the onset of puberty rather than being born with them. Most people, however, seem to have been born with a correspondence between their chromosomes, their genitalia and their respective gender identity, making it easier for them to adapt to the expectations of society. But to say that everybody who diverges from this rule is an aberration does not take into account the enormous diversity and beauty of sex expressed in nature.

In almost every living species on this planet there exists a continuum between sexes, with the lines of biological sex being blurred frequently. We may think of coral reef fish and frogs, who can change their biological sex if need be, or of the hyena whose males and females are often totally indistinguishable, due to the pseudo-penis that the female hyena possesses. Some people may find it a bit preposterous of me to refer to fish and frogs while discussing gender amongst humans. But such examples are necessary in a world where it is repeatedly claimed that a gender binary and heterosexuality are a constant of nature. Neither are. The wide range both of sexualities, sexual bodies and gender identities amongst human beings is just another manifestation of this diversity.

I have sometimes heard the argument that the issues of a few minorities—i.e. transgender people and intersex people—should not affect the way the majority of people think about gender. But that is a misjudgement. In fact, it is important to realise that who is counted as part of a minority and who is not is also culturally defined. Just as some traditional South Asian societies arbitrarily define who is a 'real woman' and who is not, the lines drawn by modern Western societies are often not less arbitrary. This becomes nowhere as apparent as in modern medical definitions of who is regarded as intersex and who is not. In this context, the idea that intersex people always possess both full male and female genitalia is a misguided one; only the rarest cases meet that description. Abusive surgeries, however, are performed on a far wider range of people. I have already mentioned that the word 'intersex' actually encompasses a broad range of physical conditions related to genitalia, chromosomes, hormones and secondary sex characteristics and it is actually a matter of quite random human decision that we draw lines neatly separating 'normal bodies' from 'intersex bodies'. The way these lines are sometimes drawn remind one of the ways colonial officials drew border lines of subject nations.

In fact, the precise definition of what constitutes a 'sexually ambiguous body' may differ from culture to culture and time period to time period. I have already mentioned that some cultures have believed that all human bodies are sexually ambiguous at birth and that customs such as the circumcision of boys or female genital mutilation are often justified with the logic that the removal of foreskin or a protruding clitoris would render the body less ambiguous. That such logics are not so far away from our own can be observed in the surgical violence that the West still regularly inflicts on the bodies of new born intersex people but also in the unease that we, as societies, feel around penises that seem too small or with labia or a clitoris that seems too large. In fact, clitoral reduction surgery or labia correction, not for medical reasons but out of a desire to 'look normal', is still a fairly common medical procedure in many Western hospitals. We have a very normative idea of how male and female genitalia should look and it is not only many intersex and transgender people but also many cisgender people who do not fit into that narrow perception of what is normal.

I find it quite astonishing that trans exclusionary feminists do not seem to realise that their insistence on reducing female identity to the existence of specific reproductive organs runs into problems when tested against the incompatibility of that normativity with a lot of human realities. What do we make of women, for example, who were born with a vagina and who identify as women but who discover during puberty that they are unable to menstruate, are born without a uterus and possess XY chromosomes? Such cases may be very rare, but they do exist. Given that they are considered socially taboo, we can expect that these cases are also less rare than reported. I assume that most trans exclusionary radical feminists would probably say that such a woman is nevertheless still a woman. While TERFs do not reduce female identity to reproductive organs as such, they hold that having certain reproductive organs and other physical markers gives one a specific experience of gender in life and makes one an object of misogyny and discrimination. I agree to this extent, but where exactly do we draw the line?

During the first part of my life I experienced marginalisation and discrimination because I was a feminine child who did not fulfil the expectations that society had for boys. I have spent the second, greater part of my life experiencing misogyny as a visible woman. I have, perhaps, experienced misogyny differently to a cisgender woman. There are different ways of being an object of social and cultural misogyny. Neither I nor a cisgender woman could be said to have experienced the same difficulties as intersex women, for example. Ultimately, though, we all suffer from the same system which privileges the cisgender male heterosexual experience above all others. I do not think that transphobia can ever be divorced from misogyny. Transmisogyny is, in essence, an expression of hate for everything female and feminine. That is how it is voiced and how it is constructed. As such, as a transgender woman in Western society, I am first and foremost discriminated against because of institutional misogyny.

Furthermore, I would hold that being a 'transgender woman' is as much a problematic and culturally contested category as the category of 'woman' as such. If we set up a binary between 'transgender women' on the one hand and 'cisgender women' on the other, we imply that all cisgender women have the same or at least very similar experiences of gender and how that gender relates to privilege. We also imply that the same is true for 'transgender women'. But here again, things are at least as murky as the realities of biological sex. I have mentioned the necessity for all of us to question our own privileges and I am more than willing to question what kind of privileges have been given to me due to the fact I was assigned male at birth. It is possible that some teachers may have treated me better at school, for example, though I can remember only few instances where this was apparent.

The first ten years of my life I was regularly bullied and belittled for being too feminine. In the second decade of my life I was taught by society to feel deep shame about my femininity and my sexuality while I was struggling with my body changing in painful ways. The following twenty years of my life I have lived as a woman and have experienced what it means to be discriminated against as a woman. When walking home alone late at night I keep my keys in my hand in case I need them as a weapon to defend myself. In the many cases where I have been sexually assaulted, I have felt the same petrifying shame that my cisgender female friends tell me they have experienced. I have been, additionally, in those situations always terribly afraid that my harasser could discover that I am transgender, because not unfrequently do such discoveries lead to the murder of transgender women.

For my whole life, then, I have had very clear experiences of both misogyny and transphobia. Needless to say, this experience is different from the experience of Caitlyn Jenner, who spent more than forty-five years of her life as a wealthy and successful athlete. Between Caitlyn and me, there are thousands of other ways of experiencing being a transgender woman; we do not all have the same relationship with male privilege. Neither do all cisgender women. I have known cisgender women, for example, who identify clearly as women but who have a very androgynous or even masculine appearance and who have sometimes been misgendered as male. One such acquaintance once told me that at times she had not corrected this misgendering when she had felt that it had given her some benefit in life. Does this momentary participation in male privilege make this woman any less of a woman?

Expecting that trans women should go to male public bathrooms puts them in danger of transphobic and sexual violence. I do not understand how that could ever be considered part of any feminist agenda. The argument of TERFs is that transgender women are men who invade female spaces and are therefore a possible source of sexual violence. Sexual violence can be perpetrated by all human beings, however. There have been transgender women who have been perpetrators of sexual violence; cisgender women have also committed acts of sexual violence. However, within the prevailing patriarchal structures of most societies, the far greater statistical reality is that of men raping women, including transgender women. I know very few transgender women who have not suffered from experiences of sexual violence inflicted on them by men in some way or another and I know several sisters who have been subjected to rape several times in their lives. Not rarely does sexual violence against transgender women also end in murder. In the US alone, thirty-one transgender people were murdered between January and September 2020. No matter what a given woman's views on gender and womanhood may be, how a woman can call herself a 'feminist' and still want to expose transgender people to the danger of such misogynistic sexual violence is beyond me.

Despite my rejection of the reductive, binary and violent discourse of trans exclusionary feminism, I do hold, however, that it offers us a great chance to better reflect on the realities of gender and initiate a conversation both on what it means to be a woman and what it means to be transgender in this world. In Chapter 2, I elaborated on discovering the privileges I held as a white European and mentioned that this discovery came late because I was focusing on my own marginalisation. Perhaps something similar is at play when trans exclusionary feminists are blind to the realities of transgender women. Some of these women have fought for decades against a patriarchal system that has disadvantaged them severely.

It has not been too long since a wife had to ask her husband for permission to be able to earn her own money in countries such as the US, the UK or Germany. Likewise, marital rape was considered legal up until fairly recently, with English criminal law only overturning its legality in 1991. Issues such as the rights of women to their own bodies remain contested and women still remain highly disadvantaged in many sectors of society. That there has been progress in that regard is only thanks to the fight of the feminist movement. But this has also meant that many women have turned this fight into the pole around which their whole identity and self-conception turns. Just as I did as a young person, these women have learned to solely understand themselves as marginalised subjects. In that position it is very difficult to question your own privileges, as realising that you also have privileges and that you also oppress and marginalise others makes you morally vulnerable. The aggressiveness with which TERFs assert their own views is, therefore, not surprising.

On the other hand, I also think that the aggressiveness of some trans activists is rooted in a very similar experience. Fighting for the acceptance of their own gender identity has likewise turned them into dogmatists. Their own sense of themselves has been threatened and attacked throughout their lives and it is no surprise that they feel the need to defend it forcefully and without questioning. We therefore now have a discourse in which two antagonistic forces insist on focusing on their own experience of marginalisation alone and that has left us with very reductive descriptions of the experience of gender in our world.

Do traditional South Asian conceptions suggest a less reductive understanding of gender? Certainly not. But observing that these conceptions have a consistent internal logic that is at the same time very different from the logic of our own ideas may lead us towards a more global understanding of gender that can embrace different understandings of being a woman or being transgender within Western society.

Coming from such a global understanding I would say that there is no contradiction between me understanding myself as a *khwajasara* in a specific South Asian context while also insisting on being taken seriously as a woman in other contexts. In both cases the point is one of creating safety and empowerment.

Despite the marginalisation and discrimination that *khwajasaras* face in South Asia, there is still in this community the sense of a glorious past, a sacred presence, a specific space in society. This space also extends into the private sphere where there is a chance of experiencing love and intimacy without being trapped in fetishist desires or men's fears about their own sexuality.

In that context, the specific social space of *khwajasaras* and *hijras*, traditionally neither seen as men nor women, serves as an important counterweight to social marginalisation. We do not have any established space like that in Europe, though some people have been arguing for non-binary identities and third-gender identities to be acknowledged in the West. In Germany, since 2018, there has been an official third gender entry on legal records, largely restricted to intersex people who want to identify as non-binary. These concepts are not organic in German society, however, and they will take a long time to become so. In such a context, not acknowledging my femininity and restricting me to the male space in society is an insult. It is deeply disrespectful. And, as pointed out above, it is violent.

Granted, this topic has entered a new phase of global negotiation now. Just as some people in the West are now embracing non-binary identities, many young transgender people in South Asia do not want to be seen as traditional *khwajasaras* anymore but find the Western idea of a transgender woman or transgender man more appealing. These young people have their own good reasons for why they think this offers them new avenues that the older and more traditional concepts do not. Not rarely, the difference is one of social class: traditional *hijra* and *khwajasara* houses, in India even more so than in Pakistan, are still dominated by people who come from low-income and lower-class and caste backgrounds. Many young transgender women of the urban Indian and Pakistani upper-middle classes cannot identify much with the lived realities of these people and relate more to images of transgender women in the international media.

We need to talk in depth about specific contexts and the subtleties of discourse here. Is a 'third gender option', as in South Asia, better for transgender people than the binary that is still dominant in Western societies? For some people it is, for some it is not. The same is true vice versa. We will never be able to find an understanding of gender that will fit all. But we need to keep the discussion open and, while doing so, make sure that everybody is protected from insult, humiliation and violence.

What makes this especially difficult is that, even beyond the transgender discourse, we have, all over the world, become societies that do not hold uniform ideas on gender anymore. It is easy to define womanhood in a society in which it is absolutely clear which specific social roles, which work and which duties are essential to womanhood and which to manhood. But such cultural 'knowledge' has become widely superfluous in most Western societies and is increasingly becoming so in many segments of South Asian societies as well. Cisgender women now hold widely differing and sometimes contradictory notions of what it means to be a woman. Some of these notions may still be tied to traditional ideas, many more less so.

For many cisgender women their reproductive biology occupies a central space in their own conception of 'being a woman'. But cisgender women who have never menstruated due to health issues or who have had to go through a hysterectomy at some point in their life often find ways to understand their womanhood differently. One can easily say 'I feel like a woman' (as in Shania Twain's well-known song) but no single human being would ever be able to fully explain what those words specifically mean to her. Leyla just feels like Leyla. She may not feel like her cisgender friend but she also may not feel like her transgender friend either. 'Feeling like a woman' is an elusive and abstract concept, not only for transgender women but also for cisgender women. It is not always intelligible or conveyable. The words of

Simone de Beauvoir still hold true: 'One is not born, but rather becomes, a woman.'

Instead of constantly trying to agree—across individual experiences and opinions and across cultures—on a universal definition of womanhood, I would much prefer it if we started to think of gender as a dynamic continuum that encompasses many options. On that continuum we find experiences that are clearly coded as male or female, according to the values of specific societies (and what defines these categories may differ from society to society). But the continuum also holds enough space for all other possible identities. If you believe that your reproductive organs form an integral part of your inner sense of being a woman, then there is a space for that; this is equally the case if you believe that your inner sense of being a woman has nothing to do with your genitalia. If your inner sense tells you that sometimes you feel more of a woman and sometimes more of a man, there is space for that as well. Why should we always understand our own specific experience of gender as automatically delegitimising all other experiences?

However, when cisgender anxieties lead people to advocate for insult, humiliation and violence against transgender people, then that cannot be a part of the same conversation. In contrast, if people want to make space for both their fears and worries and my fears and worries in order to try to find a way in which all of these can be addressed, then building a future is possible. As my friend Tawseef Khan once remarked, 'As a basic rule, I believe in more spaces, not less.' I very much agree with that sentiment. We can acknowledge that there are different ways of being a woman and that includes cisgender and transgender women.

If Western feminism seems to be divided right now over its solidarity with transgender people, there is no such ambiguity to be found in the solidarities forged between the transgender movement and the feminist struggle in South Asia. In recent years, on

International Women's Day in March, I have seen more and more prominent transgender activists and *khwajasara* gurus come out in support of Pakistan's feminist 'Aurat March' (Women's March). In 2019 in particular, I saw many of my transgender and *khwajasara* sisters march with thousands of cisgender women in Karachi, Islamabad and Lahore, fighting against such issues as legal discrimination, forced marriage, frequent misogynistic acid attacks, rape and other violence against women.

In some places, the march was besieged by religious extremists who viewed the demands of the women as a sign of 'shamelessness' and an 'insult to Islam'. The extremists attacked the marching women with sticks and stones. But that did not deter the protesters in any way. On the other side of the border, in February 2019, many transgender women and *hijras* joined the protests held by Muslim women in Shaheen Bagh, Delhi, aimed against the anti-Muslim Citizenship Amendment Act of the Modi government, which systematically renders women more vulnerable to being stripped of their rights and citizenship.

I doubt that in the course of any of these protests cisgender women questioned transgender women's use of the female bathroom. Trans-exclusionary concerns in the West (and more recently among some upper-class feminists in South Asia as well) seem rather to be proverbial 'first world problems' compared to the realities of countries where women, cisgender and transgender together, are still fighting for many basic rights that are already taken for granted in most Western societies. I see the real power of feminism in these places where cisgender women and transgender people of differing identities can join together in solidarity with the aim of battling the brutality of misogyny. A lot of our discussions in the West, on the other hand, seem rather to sabotage the real strength of feminism.

7

LET'S TALK ABOUT SEX

THE SERIES *MULLAH NASRUDDIN* used to be particularly beloved amongst Indian children in the 1990s. The main character of the series was a jester and wise man known all over the Muslim world by similar names: as Nasreddin Hoca in Turkey, as Guha in Egypt and as Molla Nasruddin in the Persian-speaking world. The screenplay was based on the stories of the Russian writer Leonid Solovyov, who had collected stories about Nasruddin in Central Asia in the 1950s; it was therefore also set in Islamicate Central Asia. Despite its Central Asian setting, the series contained a couple of South Asian idiosyncrasies. One of the most remarkable of these was its depiction of court eunuchs, who were presented in a similar way to how *hijras* and *khwajasaras* are often imagined in Hindi cinema.

A number of times in the series we see the main *khwajasara* at court acting as a go-between for a corrupt ruler and the woman he desires. There is one particular scene in which the ruler asks the *khwajasara* to engage in this duty and the *khwajasara*, trying to assure him of his seductive charms, caresses the chest hair of the half-naked ruler and coos, 'Which woman would not submit to a lady-killer like you?' This scene was probably supposed to make the audience laugh. But when I first saw it—the series has remained popular since the 1990s and has been aired on Indian state television a few times—I was quite astonished. Here there was a quite open depiction of the sexuality of the *khwajasara*, who seemed to flirt quite obviously with the ruler—and in a series made for children! It is true that the children watching the series would not have been fully aware of the implications of that scene, but any attendant parent certainly would have.

Such hints at *khwajasara* and *hijra* sexuality are rare in South Asian television and cinema but they are not completely unheard of. Another example can be found in the 1986 Muzaffar Ali film *Anjuman*, set in a decaying Muslim Lucknow. Naubahaar Bua, the *hijra* character, works in the home of one of the families whom the plot is built around. In one scene, she tells a group of giggling girls how 'when she was still in the prime of her youth', she wrecked the home of a *nawab* who had become infatuated with her. Since Naubahaar Bua is clearly not in the prime of her youth anymore, this scene is probably also supposed to serve as comic relief to some extent. However, at a later point in the film, her story is confirmed as accurate and we find that Naubahaar Bua did indeed once seduce a young *nawab*, causing quite a family drama. Again, we have an unusual public admission of the sexuality of *hijras* and the fact that the objects of this sexuality are usually men who identify as straight and are married to cisgender women.

I often contrast these portrayals with conversations that I have had during my talks and workshops which address the sexuality of *khwajasaras* and *hijras* as well as the romantic relationships they engage in. When my audience is a mainstream European one, people are often quite astonished by the idea that in conservative Muslim societies in South Asia transgender women and other genderqueer people could have such fulfilled sexual and romantic lives. Often, young, cisgender, heterosexual Pakistanis and Indians, particularly women who come from urban upper-middle-class backgrounds, are no less surprised when they hear about these things. They are, of course, aware of the fact that in South Asian societies, just as in every other society, there exist sexual minorities with sex lives. That these sex lives could have any relation to their own families and social circles, however, is something that they often find difficult to imagine.

When Muzaffar Ali made *Anjuman*, he apparently had a more realist image of *hijra* sexuality in mind. The world of Lucknowi *nawabs* he depicts in the movie is one that he himself grew up in. Had he heard stories similar to that of Naubahaar Bua's romantic exploits when growing up? It is quite possible. There used to be a time when such stories were not considered anything unusual amongst the urban Muslim classes of South Asia. Zia Jaffrey tells us one of these stories from the 1950s, which, apparently, had once been widely known in the erstwhile princely state of Hyderabad.[1] Two princes related to the royal family of the Nizam of Hyderabad had fallen in love with a *hijra* dancer named Rahman, who was renowned for her beauty. The issue led to much jealousy between the two brothers, eventually causing one brother to stab the other, creating quite a scandal amongst Hyderabadi elites. The way Jaffrey tells this story, and the way it has been told to me by others, conveys no hint whatsoever that the event as such was perceived to be very unusual. Falling in love with a *hijra* dancer was not considered anything strange for a Muslim prince, although it were better if it did not lead to a knife fight between brothers.

In fact, there are several examples in the history of the sub-continent of well-known *hijra* lovers of Muslim rulers. The most famous and infamous of these examples is probably Malik Kafur, the eunuch lover and general of Delhi Sultan Alauddin Khalji. The 2018 film *Padmaavat*, in general a production of noteworthy historical inaccuracy, depicts Alauddin Khalji as a barbarous Afghan Hun and Malik Kafur as someone whom the audience probably read as a gay man. In reality, Malik Kafur was most probably a *hijra* and not a castrated man, since we know that he had not been bought from abroad but was originally a Hindu from Gujarat praised for his feminine beauty. Kafur was the person most beloved by Alauddin Khalji, most certainly more beloved than the entirely fictional Padmaavat.

The attentive student of South Asian history will therefore be aware that throughout the period Richard M. Eaton has christened the Persianate Age of India—approximately 1000 to 1800 CE—men of the Muslim upper class of South Asia engaged quite frequently in romantic and sexual relationships with *hijras*. We have already seen that such relationships were not necessarily unique to Muslim South Asia. In Chapter 3, I quoted the scholar al-Tha'alibi (d. 1038 CE) commenting on both the 'womanly and docile' and 'manly and warlike' qualities of the eunuchs of the Mamluk court in Egypt. Such a description would very much fit Alauddin Khalji's lover and general Malik Kafur. Not rarely in the many different local contexts of the past Muslim world were eunuchs and *mukhannathun* singled out as objects of male romance and sexuality.

What old stories, historical sources and even some few movies admit openly is talked about in hushed ways today, however. That does not mean that *hijras* and *khwajasaras* are any less the focus of romantic and sexual desires today than they used to be in the past, however. In fact, one of the things that struck me when I first spent time in the *hijra* community in India was that almost every single *hijra* I knew had several male admirers and at least one steady partner while, at the same time, almost every Western transgender woman I knew was single and struggled tremendously with finding a partner. This has not changed much in the years since, though it seems that relationships have now become slightly more normalised for transgender women in the West. When I started to engage with the Pakistani transgender community in 2007, I found that things there were pretty much the same as in India, in many ways even better. Several of my Pakistani *khwajasara* friends in particular have maintained quite stable long-term relationships with their partners.

It is this which usually causes the most astonishment when I talk about my experiences in South Asia to a white European audience. The idea that Islamic societies in general, and Muslim men in particular, are sexually repressed pervades a whole range of Western publications and media productions, forming a central element of right-wing discourse which depicts Muslim men as sexually unemancipated beings, ticking time bombs that sooner or later will explode in a firework of sexual harassment and rape directed at white European women. As a transgender woman, however, I must say that I generally find white European men far more sexually repressed than any Muslim men I have ever encountered romantically or sexually, in South Asia or elsewhere.

Many Western men are beset by terrible hang-ups about their sexual attraction to transgender women. They constantly wonder what such attraction may mean for their own sexuality and identity and are perpetually afraid that their fellow cisgender heterosexual male friends may find out about their desires and think that they are gay. In contrast, I have never witnessed such hang-ups with any Muslim man that I have dated or been in a relationship with. While violence against transgender women, *khwajasaras* and *hijras* unfortunately does remain a problem in South Asia (just as misogynist violence in general), I have almost never in that context heard of the perpetrators employing the so-called 'gay panic' or 'trans panic' defence that is routinely employed in cases of transphobic violence in the West: the idea that a straight man might snap when finding out that the woman he felt attracted to is 'actually a man' and that therefore homicide in such situations may be a plausible reaction.

How much more sexually repressed can one get than thinking that a mere encounter with a transgender woman could make a man question his sexual orientation and identity and may even lead him to kill that woman? It is not only Western men who find it difficult to accept that a straight man may be able to fall in love with a transgender woman or feel sexual desire for her, however, but also many Western women. On a couple of occasions, cisgender female acquaintances of mine have asked me questions that have indicated that they thought my own partner must be homosexual. These acquaintances seem to believe that a man would not have sex with a beautiful woman merely because she was not born with a vagina. It is possible that if we are viewed as having a homosexual relationship then I am not seen as a threat to them. The realisation that not a single man I have ever had sex with was gay, indeed the realisation that their own husbands and boyfriends may secretly have had sex with transgender women, could give rise to very uncomfortable anxieties in these women. Such concerns only rarely seem to exist among Muslims in South Asia.

What leads many observers to think of men in traditional Muslim societies as sexually repressed is the fact that relationships between straight-identifying, cisgender men and transgender women, *khwajasaras* and *hijras*, just as relationships between such men and other men, often occur while these men are married to cisgender women with whom they father children. Social pressures in a lot of traditional South Asian Muslim societies demand that a man should get married to a cisgender woman and start a family and for many young men there is no way around that. This is a conception of life, however, that runs contrary to the Western idea of a liberated sexuality. Hence, what these South Asian Muslim men do is understood as hypocritical by some Western proponents of the LGBT movement and their supporters. A man who leads such a life is not only dishonest to his own sexuality, he is also dishonest to a suffering wife who can only endure the secret sex life of her husband.

I do indeed know of some cases which fit such a characterisation. Some men in South Asia do lead irresponsible double lives, just as many men in the West do. I equally do not wish to skip over the fact that there are a lot of betrayed wives who suffer tremendously from the hypocrisy according to which there is less freedom for their own sexual desires than those of their philandering husbands. It is naive, however, to think that all South Asian Muslim men who have relationships with *hijras* or *khwa-jasaras* are that irresponsible. In fact, I know of many cases, both in India and Pakistan, in which the wife of the respective man knew about her husband's other relationship and was quite fine with it. I have even encountered cases where the husband's *hijra* lover became a part of the same household as his wife, who was happy to have someone else at her side to help her with household tasks and raising the children. Such arrangements are more common amongst lower social classes but they are not uncommon at all.

I do not want to discount the struggles that my South Asian sisters are going through in search of love and physical intimacy. I have known several Indian and Pakistani sisters who have been in terribly abusive relationships and others who have had their hearts broken when their boyfriend had to agree to a family-arranged marriage. Many have experienced sexual violence of all possible degrees. And still, on average, finding both love and physical intimacy is far easier for a Pakistani *khwajasara* than it is for the average trans woman in Europe. There is a reason why the vast majority of my Pakistani *khwajasara* friends and acquaintances are in long-term relationships while the vast majority of my Western trans acquaintances are not. There is also a reason why my own partner of four years grew up in a village in the Punjab: my previous dating life in Germany has been most difficult, not to say traumatic at times.

Something which has always been particularly difficult about dating in the West, for me and many other transgender women, is the strong fetishisation of our bodies. Men in the West may often worry about the integrity of their own sexual orientation or about what their pals may say about them when they discover an attraction to transgender women, but they still seek out women like us because they believe that our bodies will provide them with a special kick that neither cisgender women nor gay men can offer. The fetishist reality of trans dating in the West also affects the issue of gender reassignment. As a transgender woman, you are the object of a very specific desire as long as you remain physically a 'shemale', a 'chick with a dick'. You are something special, unique and exotic that entices men. But as soon as you undergo gender reassignment surgery, you lose that special asset (in a very literal way). At the same time, many men do not view transgender women with vaginas as eligible for an official relationship, as they still fear that their sexuality could be questioned.

I know several trans women who have hoped that after gender reassignment surgery the experience of constant fetishisation would end and they could finally have relationships with men, just like any other woman, only to discover that they have become even less desirable than before. The Netflix series *Pose*, set in New York's Black and Latino queer ballroom community of the 1980s, featured this topic in one of its storylines. The reigning queen of the ballroom, Elektra, played by Dominique Jackson, loses her rich sugar daddy boyfriend immediately after going through gender reassignment surgery. Many trans viewers of the series saw this outcome coming, since we have all heard the same story often enough from trans friends and acquaintances and some of us have experienced it ourselves. Even many decades after the 1980s, it is still a very common experience for trans women who date men. Faced with such realities, we might ask: which experience of sexuality seems more liberated? For transgender women, at least for transgender women who date men, the project of sexual liberation in the West has not really delivered what it once promised.

Many Western governments and LGBT activists in the Global South have, nevertheless, come to believe very strongly that they know best which kind of sexual practice is moral and right and which ideas should be exported to the rest of the world as well. They have come to believe that Islamic societies are not only deeply oppressive towards sexual minorities but that these societies even have a fundamentally incorrect understanding of what it means to be LGBT: they constantly mix up trans with intersex and gay; they equate being gay with being feminine and with the sexually passive 'female' role; and straight-identified men in these societies act hypocritically because they have sex with gay and trans-identified individuals without coming out themselves. In the eyes of the West, a huge number of such straight men in Muslim societies are actually 'closet gays' who are in denial about their own sexuality.

The archetype invoked, that of the repressed homosexual man who victimises his wife, always supposes that a relationship with a man or a transgender woman is somehow morally worse than one with a cisgender heterosexual woman. The problem here is the hypocrisy with which the sexuality of transgender women as much as male homosexuality is judged, a hypocrisy which in itself betrays issues of sexual repression in Western societies. The fact that such essentially homophobic and transphobic ideas are preached as part of an ideology that purportedly stands for sexual liberation is quite disappointing. Similarly disappointing is the lack of critical awareness that the representatives of this discourse have when it comes to the culturally and historically situated character of their own identities and sexual orientations. I have already bemoaned, in the case of some trans activists, the way that sexuality is thought about in very dogmatic ways which do not allow us to understand that our categories of sexual orientation and gender identity are just as constructed as the categories of traditional South Asian societies. In fact, the categories we are familiar with nowadays are all relatively new and imperfect, their precise definitions constantly in flux.

Historical studies such as George Chauncey's *Gay New York* and Hugh Ryan's *When Brooklyn was Queer* show that, until recently, male sexuality as practised in the big urban centres of the West was often understood in very similar ways to how it is still understood in parts of South Asian Muslim society today. This was especially true for the working classes. In the early twentieth century, working-class gay men in cities such as New York, London and Berlin would have found the idea that gay men were supposed to have sex with each other ridiculous. Gay-identified men would seek out straight-identified men and would often play a passive sexual role whilst doing so—or at least pretended to the outside world that they did—in order to enact femininity and not disturb their partner's sense of social identity. In that setting, what we would call 'gay' and what we would call 'trans' was part of a continuum. Sexuality was intrinsically tied to gendered performance. There were also men who had sex with other men who would not abide by such a gendered performance, but these men mostly identified as straight as well. They saw no need to tie their sexual behaviour to a specific sexuality or identity; they merely saw sexual relief as a basic need such as food or oxygen which could be fulfilled with anybody at any time.

Our world has changed considerably since then and so have our concepts of sexuality. When we see a lot of these patterns, once very common in our own urban Western centres, in majority Muslim countries, we consider them strange and see them as signs of 'unliberated sexuality'. Nevertheless, remnants of the older narratives surrounding sexuality were still very much alive when I was growing up. I remember that one of the most common LGBT themes in films and soap operas back then was the story of the gay man unhappily in love with a straight man. People at that time still took it for granted that this was how things should be.

This kind of storyline rarely appears nowadays. Gay men are seen as finally where they belong, in their own little community where they can love as they want to, no longer a threat to straight families and heterosexual integrity. Even the 'bisexual' has been rendered to his own corner. It is remarkable that in the early twentieth century Sigmund Freud still held the idea that every human being is essentially bisexual. This idea was widely popular in many LGBT circles up until the 1990s, but it has ever since been almost completely replaced with the 'born this way' idea: that sexual orientations are essential and unchangeable and something we are all born with. People who nevertheless do explicitly identify as bisexual are often shunned or at least not taken seriously both in many gay and straight circles (even though the 'B' is always mentioned when it comes to acronyms).

Sigmund Freud's once very popular assertion deserves more attention, however. When, in 1948, Alfred Kinsey and his associates published the Kinsey Report, *Sexual Behaviour in the Human Male*, they found that the vast majority of men in the US expressed homosexual desires and had had homosexual experiences to at least some degree. Kinsey furthermore determined that the sexuality of most men exists on a spectrum between 'pure homosexuality' and 'pure heterosexuality'. This spectrum was measured on the so-called 'Kinsey scale'. Kinsey contended that the sexuality of most men would be somewhere in the middle, between the blocks of 'pure homosexuality' and 'pure heterosexuality', sometimes tending more to one side, sometimes to the other. Kinsey's method of sampling has been critiqued since, but his basic premise seems to give us a good impression of male sexuality in the United States of the 1940s and 1950s. His quantitative findings are also corroborated by what we know from more recent qualitative studies of the sexuality of those times, such as the above-mentioned works of Chauncey and Ryan.

Kinsey's work opened up a discussion on sexuality in Western societies that eventually helped to advance LGBT freedoms considerably. His study demonstrated that homosexual desires were to a large degree 'normal' and found in most human beings and were, therefore, not pathological at all. Strangely though, along-side the gains of LGBT movements, the idea that the sexuality of most men exists on a spectrum seems to have become taboo. Not only do we now confine legitimate sexual behaviour to specific sexual identities, but we also see that the more space that exists in society for homosexual identities, the less many men admit their own homosexual desires and experiences. If Kinsey tried to collect his data nowadays, I suspect he would probably discover far more prevalent binary blocks of 'pure homosexuality' and 'pure heterosexuality' than he did in the, allegedly, far more repressive 1940s and 1950s.

What we see here is that across the course of the twentieth century, an orthodoxy on sexuality emerged in Western societies which suppressed spectrum and continuum. Straight-identified men who secretly fulfil desires for sex and intimacy with men, transgender women and queer people are a nightmare for modern post-Kinsey society. We therefore created a socially acceptable script for homosexual desires. If you sever your ties with straight social life, come out publicly and accept a certain identity, then your sexuality is deemed acceptable. If you don't, then you are a hypocrite and sexually repressed.

Sexual desires and social comfortability are never easily negotiable, though. Recent studies of the consumption of pornography provide some revealing insights here. Not only is, in all societies, the demand for homosexual and transgender pornography much higher than the social acceptance of gay men and transgender women would lead one to believe, but there is, apparently, also a huge pornographic market for categories such as 'old fat hairy women'. The very same men who regularly search for such porn entries will usually choose a very different partner for their married social life. In essence, the pattern is essentially the same as that of straight-identifying men who secretly pursue their homosexual desires. Due to our constructs of 'sexual orientation', however, we morally judge one case far more severely than the other.

Another unexpected genre enjoying quite a bit of popularity nowadays is 'tentacle pornography'. This genre may strike some modern Western readers as quite pathological, and certainly only few people would casually admit to enjoying it, although it started out as a pretty respectable form of erotica in eighteenth-century Japan, best known through the early nineteenth-century *shunga* painting 'The Dream of the Fisherman's Wife' which depicted a woman having sexual intercourse with a giant octopus. Would we ever demand that a person dedicated to these kind of fantasies should leave their spouse and children, publicly come out as a tentacle-lover and marry an octopus? Would we call them a hypocrite or sexually repressed if they didn't? Probably not.

Our societies are apparently not very well equipped to deal with the complexities of human sexuality, romance and desire for intimacy. Our discourses cannot accept spectrums, continuums and shades of grey. Instead, we seek solace from our anxieties in the comforting ghettos of 'sexual orientation' and 'identity'. Even more so, we demand that others seek refuge in these ghettos so that their ambiguous desires may not cause us any fears or anxieties. In that sense, modern Western societies are not much better than those characterised as stereotypically hyper-patriarchal and homophobic. We all enact a social engineering of sexuality aimed towards repressing what may be seen as culturally uncomfortable.

The price of such social engineering is always high and it is debatable how far these ideas of freedom are benefitting those who subscribe to them. Finding a partner in the gay community has become a terrible game of status that is weighing down heavily on the mental health of many gay men. Racism abounds in the community and it has taken a toll on the mental health of many gay people of colour in Western societies. There is a shockingly high number of gay men who have internalised fear of and hate for their own femininity and the femininity of other men and who suffer from body dysphoria.

Recent studies show that dramatically high numbers of gay men suffer from mental stress, depression and anxiety disorders compared to the rest of the population. The numbers of suicides and suicide attempts by gay men are also disproportionately high. Risky drug abuse is rampant and, in the so-called chemsex scene, is tied to equally risky sexual behaviour. There have been a couple of studies showing that even in European countries where social acceptance of homosexuality is high (e.g. Sweden) these factors still persist. It is not simply mainstream society's lack of tolerance that puts mental pressure on gay men, then. The resumé shows that, even with all of the freedoms we have fought for over so many decades, gay men in the West, as a social group, are a deeply unhappy population with a high mortality rate.

What is worse is that a large part of the gay community is in vocal denial of this fact and would prefer to continue its happy narrative of sexual authenticity, emancipation and freedom—a narrative exported to the rest of the world. The tragedy for many gay men is that they often grow up feeling like they cannot be themselves. Coming out is supposed to liberate oneself from the pain that that constant trauma brings. But then, many men find that they cannot be themselves within the gay community either.

If you are too feminine, then you have to man up.

I anticipate objection to what I have just written. A trans woman trashing the gay community? That is not the position I am writing from; rather, I write as a person who still comes from a generation when gay and trans communities were much more intertwined and related. We are very much mirror images of each other, the gay discourse reflecting on the trans discourse and vice versa. In many ways, we are both products of a social engineering that tried to give order to the chaotic implications of the Kinsey scale. As mentioned in Chapter 1, I once identified as gay myself at some point in my teenage years and the gay community was the first space within which I was able to explore my trans identity. I write as someone who is at least as critical of the modern Western trans narratives as of the gay narratives. Most importantly, I write as a person who wants us all to do better and to feel better.

The global multiplicity of sexuality can teach us something here. My point is not to say that this or that culture is essentially doing it better than the other. Each culture gives birth to its own monsters and produces its own kinds of repression which take their toll on human health and lives. Looking at different interpretations of sexuality and comparing them with each other may make us aware of the spaces in between that we can explore to make life better for all of us. This 'all of us' includes heterosexual and cisgender people. In the end, we are all human beings with very specific individual sexual and romantic desires, trying to find our way through this labyrinth of labels and identities.

8

CRIME AND PREJUDICE

IT WAS DURING ONE of my later stays at a *dera* in Delhi that I had an encounter which led me to question for quite a while whether I wanted to continue engaging with the *hijra* community at all. At that time, I had already been aware of conflicts between the *gharana* of my own *dera* and another *gharana*. These kind of conflicts usually erupted when there was a conflict surrounding territories that supposedly belonged to the *gharanas*. Allegedly harkening back to privileges given to specific *hijra* lines by the last Mughal emperors, each *gharana* had inherited specific rights to go on *badhai* in particular parts of the city. These rights had never been codified in the books of law of the modern state of India, of course, and thus they had no official legal basis anymore. Since the times of the Mughal emperors, however, cities like Delhi had grown considerably and so when it came to newly built quarters of the city, it was not always entirely clear which parts would fall into the territory of which *gharana*. Since such rights were tied to important issues of income and wealth, they easily led to quite serious conflict which could sometimes even break out in incidents of physical violence.

On the day of this encounter, I had been to a random photo shop to get a film developed (this was still in the time before digital cameras and smartphones). While I was waiting in the shop to receive my developed photographs, a group of *hijras* unknown to me suddenly entered and started to ask me a number of questions. It very quickly became clear that this group of *hijras* knew who I was. They must have heard about me, the 'white *hijra*'. At first, the questions they asked me only seemed to be slightly annoying. But then they became more and more aggressive and I realised that the group was forming a circle around me and that they were not looking at me in a particularly nice way.

At one point they asked me, very assertively, to come with them to their *dera*. I realised that these *hijras* must be *chelas* from the 'other' *gharana*, the one our own *gharana* was in conflict with. They either wanted to pressure me into joining their *gharana*, or they wanted to abduct me. The atmosphere became increasingly frightening and tense and I became quite worried for my own safety. Fortunately, the owner of the photo shop started to notice what was going on. He knew who I was and to which people I belonged. He called his two sons and together they managed to chase the other *hijras* away. Eventually one of his sons brought me back home on his motorbike.

In the following weeks, the conflict between the two *gharanas* erupted even more, after the incident of a shooting that became a subject of the Delhi yellow press and finally a court case. When I heard of that incident I wondered whether, that day in the photo shop, I may have been in far more danger than I realised at the time.

When I give talks and interviews about my experiences with the *hijra* community, I rarely speak about these kind of incidents. The *hijra* community is first and foremost a refuge for the marginalised and a source of solidarity for most of its members. Violence and conflict are not everyday occurrences in that community. In the eyes of the public though, violence and conflict are often emphasised, particularly in Indian and Pakistani media reports on the community where *hijra* and *khwajasara gharanas* are depicted as some kind of mafia structure that mostly thrives on illegal activities and keeps its members loyal by pressure and force alone. I am very careful not to reinforce the negative stereotypes that have been created by this kind of sensationalist media reporting and I am quite conscious of the fact that sharing my own stories of conflict and violence within the community might give credibility to these stereotypes.

Conflict does exist in the community, however, as do violence and illegal activities. The *hijra* and *khwajasara* community is not alone in this amongst marginalised communities, of course. It is somewhat of a global rule that the less a community is given space in the public sphere of a society the more it has to retreat to the shadows of not-so-public activity in order to survive. In previous chapters I have spoken about the connections between the *hijra* and *khwajasara* community and the past glories of Muslim courts. I have also spoken about the spiritual powers ascribed to members of this community and about its connection to the saints of Sufi and Shi'a Islam. All of these things structure the realities of the community, giving its members a sense of having a specific place in society and ensuring that third-gender people in South Asia have far more social visibility than trans-gender people in other parts of the world.

The importance of all of these old traditions has been fading away in recent decades, however, within the community and even more so within South Asian mainstream society. *Hijras* and *khwa-jasaras* find it more and more difficult to survive on traditional income such as *badhai*, while also facing many hurdles when it comes to entering regular non-traditional professions. Most *khwa-jasaras* and *hijras* come from family backgrounds that are very low in income and they do not have sufficient levels of education to advance enough in society to make a profitable living on their own. For many, sex work and illegal activities are the only option to survive. Therefore, the fight for dominance amongst *gharanas* has become a necessity for the *gharanas* and *deras* who, until now, relied specifically on traditional sources of income.

The process that has successively forced *hijras* and *khwajasaras* into illegality and the shadow realms of society did not begin in recent decades, of course. The foundations for this were laid with the Criminal Tribes Act of 1871, through which the government of British India criminalised a number of communities that did not fit Victorian British ideals of family and community. Amongst these communities, we find those collectively labelled as 'eunuchs', a term the British applied not only to courtly *khwajasaras* and the *badhai-hijras* but also to a number of other gender non-conforming communities. The British colonial administration outlawed activities such as public dancing and dressing in women's clothes, and they criminalised sodomy—which, by extension, referred to all sexual and romantic relationships that *hijras* had with men—and voluntary castration. The British government also required all 'eunuchs' to be officially registered and they forcibly removed all children who had grown up in *deras*.

A particular accusation against the *hijra* community became widespread under the British administration—one that is sometimes still found in the South Asian yellow press today—the idea that *hijras* regularly abduct young male children in order to forcibly castrate them and to 'turn them into *hijras*'. This idea follows a well-established European colonial pattern of accusing marginalised communities of crimes such as kidnapping children and of physically harming them, morally corrupting them or both. In medieval Europe, such accusations were often levelled against Jews. In the early modern period they were often extended to Romani and Traveller people as well. In fact, accusations of kidnapping have negatively hit Romani and Traveller communities in Greece and Ireland even in the twenty-first century. The idea, still widespread in some quarters, that gay men are synonymous with paedophiles is part of this same pattern, as are accusations that male sexual predators regularly assume the identities of transgender women to get access to children. As far as I know, there are no testimonies of such accusations ever having been levelled against *khwajasaras* and *hijras* in pre-colonial South Asia. During British colonial rule, however, they became almost commonplace and were directly tied to a regime of social and legal persecution.

Such colonial-era persecution has cast a shadow that still looms large over the community even today. Ever since, the community has been unable to fully regain the status it had occupied before. Suspicions created by Victorian administrators made a deep impact on how the educated classes of South Asia started to view *khwajasaras* and *hijras*. In fact, contrary to what one may think, it is even today often the case that it is specifically members of an educated, urban, upper-middle class in South Asia that carry the most prejudices against the community. In the lower classes and in rural areas *hijras* and *khwajasaras* still remain far more integrated into general society, perhaps because the colonial administration had a less pronounced influence on the worldviews prevalent amongst these classes.

A particularly vicious side effect of this development is that members of the community themselves are very much aware of the fact that mainstream society loves to hear gruesome sensationalist stories about violence and repression within the community and have therefore sometimes become very willing to conduct what has been called 'respectability politics'. If you want to portray yourself as a 'good *khwajasara*' or, even better, a 'good transgender woman' in the eyes of the Pakistani or Indian mainstream, your best bet is always to publicly dissociate yourself from the rumours and wild stories about the community. Many community members have done so by blaming all the suggested negative happenings of *hijra* life on other *gharanas*, other *deras* and other *hijras* while washing themselves entirely free of all of these purported sins. It has frequently been remarked by journalists and researchers alike that *hijras* often admit that many in the community engage in sex work, but, of course, this work is usually only ever done by some other *gharana* or some other *dera*. To an even greater extent, many *hijras* will admit that there are 'bad gurus' who use force and violence and may engage in illegal activities, but, unsurprisingly, these bad gurus also always belong to another *gharana*.

Ironically, these respectability politics have reached a new height since transgender, *khwajasara* and *hijra* activism took off properly in the 2010s and since *khwajasara* and *hijra* issues have been taken more seriously by South Asian mainstream societies, including remarkable advances in transgender rights in Pakistan, in particular. Ever since, it has become an even more pressing issue for many members of the community to not let these advances be spoiled by 'bad apples' amongst their own ranks. That does pose a particular problem, however, for a community that has, since colonial times, been forced into illegality and survival tactics. In such a community, the same respectability that is demanded by the non-marginalised is a rare good.

This has created a situation in the community in which mutual solidarity is often sacrificed in the name of good image. More than once I have seen members of the community publicly accuse other members, often vaguely and impersonally, of physical and sexual abuse. There have been a couple of people who have come forward to the public with such stories without naming the culprit. These accusations have gained new legitimacy in the age of the #MeToo movement and have often taken the form of very personal attacks. Sometimes these cases have become more well-known to the general public, sometimes they have remained less so, but over the course of the last ten years there have been at least three or four different cases where I have known both the accusers and the accused personally. The particular tragedy in these cases comes with the knowledge that there were, in almost all of them, incidents of violence and abuse but that, from a closer view, these stories were far more complex than those which had been presented to the public. In almost all of the cases I was aware of, the accused had usually been victims of physical and sexual abuse themselves, while many of the accusers had also been perpetrators of sexually and physically abusive behaviour.

The problem here is a structural one, not an individual one. Since its persecution in colonial times, the community has become one marked by incredible violence on many levels of its existence. Violence inflicted on the community by the outside world has created repeated manifestations of violence within the community. The cycle here is a very classic cycle of abuse. The problem of the abused who eventually becomes an abuser himself is well-known and it should come as no surprise that such cycles become established in communities that have been collective victims of abuse for generations. As the problem is a structural one, it will, therefore, need a structural solution as well. Individual respectability politics, however, only keeps the cycle of abuse and violence rolling.

The problem is also a structural one not only as far as the community's particular history of marginalisation is concerned but also in the context of the space that the community occupies today within an entire society that has itself become impacted by repeated cycles of abuse. Thanks to a legacy of colonial exploitation, political corruption, economic instability and a merciless global neoliberal capitalist system, violence and abuse have become widespread in South Asia. This manifests in numerous forms: the highly publicised gang rape cases in India and Pakistan; the murderous lynch mobs descending on alleged blasphemers in Pakistan and alleged beef eaters in India; and the countless cases of sexual abuse in both Muslim *madrasas* and Hindu *ashrams*.

India and Pakistan are countries in which the military, rich elites and religious extremists constantly inflict excruciating violence on others and are almost never held accountable for it. It is not just these societies that are to blame for this, but also the global injustices that are still sustained by postcolonial Western

171

societies. Due to this existing framework of global power structures, Western corporations are able to commit horrifying human
rights abuses in South Asia on an almost daily basis without
being held accountable. We live in and sustain a global structure
of violence and within such a structure it is ludicrous to expect a
marginalised minority in an already struggling society to be free
of such violence.

Sadly, the advent of a global LGBT movement has not made
things any easier for most transgender and other queer communities in South Asia. It has been remarked by a number of
analysts that one of the most serious scourges neoliberal capitalism has inflicted on the Global South is the NGO-isation of
social politics. The problem here is not the NGOs as such. It is
surely a good thing that all over the world organisations exist
that have dedicated themselves to fighting for human rights
issues. Both in India and Pakistan, a number of very brave activists have worked for decades within the framework of such
NGOs, through which they have often been able to effect very
real change within their societies. The problem is, however, that
many NGOs are fundamentally dependent on a neoliberal agenda
that is ultimately opposed to any actual progress in human rights
issues. In 2014, Indian writer Arundhati Roy warned us of the
devastating influence that such an agenda has had on social
movements, writing:

> Most large-funded NGOs are financed and patronized by aid and
> development agencies, which are, in turn, funded by Western gov-
> ernments, the World Bank, the UN and some multinational corpo-
> rations. Though they may not be the very same agencies, they are
> certainly part of the same loose, political formation that oversees the
> neoliberal project and demands the slash in government spending in
> the first place. Why should these agencies fund NGOs? Could it be
> just old-fashioned missionary zeal? Guilt? It's a little more than that.
> NGOs give the impression that they are filling the vacuum created

by a retreating state. And they are, but in a materially inconsequential way. Their real contribution is that they defuse political anger and dole out as aid or benevolence what people ought to have by right. They alter the public psyche. They turn people into dependent victims and blunt the edges of political resistance.[1]

For a long time, social policy experts have noted that more often than not NGOs serve as agents of both Western hegemony and neoliberal capitalism and therefore are incapable of creating any sustainable structural change that could elevate the status of marginalised minorities. In 2012, Glen W. Wright, a sustainable development researcher, wrote: 'There are two main roles that NGOs play. First, they act as softener for the damage caused by the West's structural adjustment policies in the developing world, thus lessening resistance to those policies; and second, they diffuse the grassroots political resistance to neo-liberalism.'[2] A dangerous mix.

Almost all *khwajasara, hijra* and transgender activists that I know in Pakistan and India are now working within the framework of NGOs that largely receive funding from abroad. All of them work very hard and with the best intentions. I also see that most of them have virtually no other choice but to work within the framework of these NGOs. A particularly pernicious facet of neoliberal capitalism is its creation of dependencies that are very difficult to deconstruct. Asking many *khwajasara, hijra* and transgender activists to simply step outside of NGO frameworks in this climate is essentially equivalent to asking any one of us to stop working in what the late anthropologist David Graeber has called 'bullshit jobs' and become self-sufficient by growing our own food. The idea may sound good from the perspective of a general critique of a damaged system. But almost none of us would be willing or even able to dare taking such a risk.

The individual activists who work within the NGO framework are not at fault here, but rather global policy makers, most of them from 'the West' or 'the Global North', who have created the situation at hand. Also at fault are weak civil society and militarised governments in India and Pakistan which have no interest in supplying alternative structures that could genuinely take care of human rights issues without relying on foreign donors.

Robbed of their traditional sources of income, inheriting a colonial-era legacy of marginalisation and criminalisation, many members of the *hijra* and *khwajasara* communities are now embedded in a new colonial order that constantly instigates competition between groups for resources, at times leading to rivalries far more vicious than the traditional rivalries surrounding territory. In some sense, one could say, NGOs have become the new income-oriented territories that *gharanas*, *deras* and individuals have to fight for. Here, respectability politics begins to mix with the ideological demands of foreign funders and not always in a conscious way. Foreign donors have a particular idea of what it means to be LGBTQI, what it means to be transgender and what kind of freedom sexual minorities in Muslim majority countries and South Asia would need to gain access to fundamental rights. Many of these ideas are well intentioned and some of them may even be good, but none of these ideas have much to do with the sources of wisdom and tradition that have empowered *khwajasaras* and *hijras* for centuries. Many of these ideas are also constructed in ways that antagonise parts of South Asian Muslim mainstream society. There is money and funding attached to these ideas, however, encouraging a new generation of *khwajasaras* and *hijras* to eagerly adopt them, whether they are useful or not, instead of relying on networks that have survived for far longer.

It is true that this harsh critique of the NGO-isation of LGBTQI rights politics in the Muslim world and elsewhere in the Global South needs to be checked against the lived realities of those whose lives may nevertheless experience some improvement through these ideas. In July 2020, the Egyptian queer activist Ismail Fayed published a reply to this critique in *Mada Masr*, titled 'On Queerness and the Jargon of Authenticity'. In it he very rightly scolded Muslim activists who sit comfortably in the embrace of human rights granted to them in their resident Western countries but who criticise activists in the Muslim world for allegedly not being 'culturally authentic' enough and for too easily adopting the language and concepts of the Western LGBTQI movement.

Fayed notes that these Muslim activists—myself included, I assume—too easily ignore the struggle of the everyday fight that activists in the Muslim world are leading and too easily paint them as lackeys of globalised agendas. I consider his critique of queer Muslim identity politics in the West a necessary and needed one. I would also say that the context of Pakistan is very different from the context of Egypt that Fayed addresses. The *khwajasara* community has had a very vibrant and vivid cultural life until recently and it still practises many customs of that cultural life. It would be great to see the resources of empowerment that this cultural life offers mattering as much globally as the resources of empowerment that the global LGBTQI movement extends. Issues of funding mean that this cannot presently be the case. The same issues of funding have also disrupted the social structure of *khwajasara* society to a painful extent.

9

ISLAMISM AND ISLAMOPHOBIA

IN OCTOBER 2016, A poster appeared in several public locations in Karachi claiming: 'If this was Saudi Arabia, we would behead these people.' Nobody was able to say with certainty who had created the amateurish print-outs carrying this message. But they caused concerns in some segments of Karachi's transgender and *khwajasara* communities, as the people who should be beheaded, according to this text, were *khwajasaras*. Or, rather, '*hijras*', a word intentionally deployed for the negative and politically incorrect connotations that it carried in Pakistan by then. The posters further asserted that '*hijras*' are actually men; that there was allegedly no such thing as a third gender in Islam; and that women should keep away from sinful '*hijras*'.

This poster was strange and remarkable in a Pakistani context. Never before had I heard of such views being shared by Pakistani Muslims. There had been, as mentioned before, debates on 'real' and 'fake' *khwajasaras* in Pakistani society. But South Asian Muslims in general, no matter what interpretation of Islam they followed, had never doubted that *khwajasaras* had their own place in creation and society. Many people were unsure about what exactly a *khwajasara* was, but that *khwajasaras* were not men was common knowledge. The sudden appearance of this print-out demonstrated, however, that Pakistan was also not immune to the influence of a globalised and deculturalised Islam that had adopted a modern gender binary and that considered this gender binary an intrinsic element of 'true Islam'. Such a globalised and deculturalised Islam was often preached by returning middle-class guest workers from Saudi Arabia and the Gulf States. The phrase 'if so-and-so would happen in Saudi Arabia, they would

179

cut off their heads/hands/lash them' had become a catch phrase that was often typical of such returnees.

Islamist transphobia still remains rare in Pakistan even today and raises its head only very rarely. By that I mean the clear and in-your-face transphobia that manifests itself in regular arrests of transgender people in many Arab Middle Eastern countries and that serves as the basis for the murders of transgender people committed by insurgent Islamist groups such as ISIS. When the Islamist Taliban started to gain more and more control in the North-Western regions of Pakistan in the wake of 9/11 and the US 'War on Terror', this led to a number of discriminatory measures and also increased violence against *khwajasaras* in the region. These measures were mostly directed against the entertainment and sex work provided by *khwajasaras*, however, and against appearing in public in a way that the Taliban considered unchaste. The Taliban wanted to bring an end to what they perceived as sinful activity, even though many Taliban commanders themselves secretly had *khwajasara* lovers or kept underage male sex slaves. But even the Pakistani Taliban usually did not doubt that, as such, the existence of *khwajasaras* had a certain legitimacy.

In 2018, when the Transgender Protection of Rights Bill passed the approval of the Pakistani parliament, the Jamiat Ulema-e-Islam was the strongest Islamist party in the parliament and the bill also passed the approval of Pakistan's Council of Islamic Ideology. Both had happened as the result of some negotiation and several meetings between transgender and *khwajasara* activists and members of both party and council. What is all the more remarkable is that this anti-discrimination bill insists that the identity of transgender people has to be respected according to their own self-representation and identification. The bill therefore rejects all medicalisation or biologisation of transgender rights and is, in that way, much more progressive than the transgender laws in many Western countries.

That is not to say that the existence of *khwajasaras* and other transgender people has not also worried Islamist movements in South Asia at times. But, as in the above-mentioned case concerning the Taliban, this worry was usually confined to general questions of public morality. Islamists were and are worried about *khwajasara* sex work because it is sex work, not so much because it is done by *khwajasaras*. They were and are worried about *khwajasaras* dancing as entertainers because they perceive this as lewd entertainment; whether the dancing is done by *khwajasaras* or cisgender women is not important (and many Pakistani Islamists would probably even prefer *khwajasara* dancers since, in their minds, the mythic 'honour' of cisgender women is of a much more fragile nature). But, for a long time, Pakistani Islamists have not engaged specifically with the issue of the status of *khwajasaras* in a Muslim society.

Abul A'la Maududi (d. 1979), considered by many to be the father of both Pakistani and global Islamism, seemed quite perplexed when confronted with the question of how to deal with the *khwajasara* community. In his commentary on the Holy Quran, he seemed to follow the reasoning of classical Muslim scholars that I described in Chapter 4—that is, that the Prophet had not prohibited *mukhannathun*, a category that he equated with eunuchs and *khwajasaras*, from frequenting Muslim society in general, but had only criticised those *mukhannathun* who had shown lewd and improper sexual desires. Maududi did seem to think that there were 'born eunuchs' who could not be blamed for who they were.

However, unease not only with sex work and entertainment work performed by *khwajasaras* but also with customs such as wearing make-up and feminine clothes has often become a characteristic of South Asian Islamist discourse around transgender people. In this context, between 2015 and 2020, a particularly strange phenomenon started to appear in Pakistan within the pietist Tablighi Jamaat movement and amongst the followers of the popular Sunni Deobandi preacher Tariq Jameel. A number of *khwajasaras* publicly declared their allegiance to these pietist and puritan movements, renounced wearing make-up and female clothes and started to wear the white uniform of male Deobandi aesthetics. Some even started to grow beards. This all, however, without renouncing their *khwajasara* identities as such; these pietist and fundamentalist Muslims continued to describe themselves as *khwajasaras* and 'neither male nor female'. Some also called themselves 'transgender' and continued to insist that 'God had created them this way'. A group of these pietist Muslim *khwajasaras* eventually gathered around a *khwajasara* preacher who uses the male pronoun and calls himself Ameer Khusra, a rather amusing wordplay on the name of the Indian Muslim saint Ameer Khusrau (mentioned in Chapter 5) and the Punjabi word *khusra* for *khwajasara*. Ameer Khusra always appeared very unashamed of his exaggeratedly effeminate expressions, gestures and mannerisms while at the same time spouting a long beard in the style of Deobandi Islamists and declaring his renunciation of sinful entertainment and prostitution.

Ameer Khusra and his followers caused a lot of discussion in the Pakistani *khwajasara* community. The phenomenon was a curious one, never seen before. As I have mentioned in previous chapters, it was often common for older *khwajasara* and *hijra* gurus to dress in white and don a certain ambiguous or sexually ambivalent appearance after performing the pilgrimage to Makkah. But this was never expected from younger *khwajasaras* and was considered rather strange for someone who had not reached a certain age and status. Some *khwajasaras* noted that this new pious trend could easily develop into a threat to traditional *khwajasara* culture, especially after the new movement tried to convert a few prominent *khwajasara* gurus. But many *khwajasaras* also expressed admiration for these young sisters who had dedicated themselves to religion. Many did indeed feel that this was maybe the better way to be a *khwajasara*, even though individual circumstances, such as a dependency on income as an entertainer, may prevent them from joining this movement as well. The vast majority of Pakistani *khwajasaras* would never be willing to renounce make-up and female clothes in the name of faith. However, not a few have started to believe that there is a beauty in such renunciation. It corresponds with a *khwajasara*'s conviction that what eventually makes a *khwajasara* is not clothes or make-up but a nature that was created by God.

It is interesting that a similar move towards a more conforming modern kind of religiosity can be observed amongst some Indian *hijras* as well, here more often in the context of Hinduism. The most prominent example of such an adoption of modern religiosity has been Laxmi Narayan Tripathi, perhaps the most well-known Indian transgender activist internationally. Unlike her Muslim counterparts in Pakistan, Tripathi has not renounced wearing make-up and female clothes, but she often appears in public in a style modelled upon Hindu *sadhus* and yogis. She draws on Hindu mythology that affirms her transgender identity, while the Islamic heritage of much traditional *hijra* culture is rarely visible in her public appearances. She presents herself as the spiritual leader of a sacred order of transgender Hindu ascetics (the 'Kinnar Akhada') and precisely because of that conscious staging she has drawn much attention both from adherents of Hindu nationalist politics in India and from Westerners abroad. Many Indian transgender women and *hijras* attest that she is an important influence in the progress of transgender rights in India.

There are, however, also tensions between her and the more established and traditional *hijra* houses as well as transgender activists more critical of Hindu nationalism. In 2018, Laxmi Narayan Tripathi voiced her support for the construction of a Hindu temple on the site of the Babri Mosque in Ayodhya that was destroyed by Hindu nationalists in 1992. Her vocal support immediately drew the criticism of other *hijras*. A statement that was at that time released by a collective of 183 trans, intersex and gender nonconforming individuals, 20 LGBTQI groups, 8 ally organisations and 146 individual allies, read: 'Laxmi Narayan Tripathi's position negates the politics of communal harmony that is espoused by Hijras and Kinnars, who have historically maintained a syncretic faith of belonging to both Hinduism and Islam. It idealises a mythical past of the Sanatan Dharam and supports the right-wing politics of communal hatred.'

I had witnessed the rise of a more consciously Hindu *hijra* identity in India in 2005, but back then it was merely a matter of survival in the public sphere. While in our house the dominant religious influence was Islam, in a form that allowed for syncretic mixing with Hindu elements, some of my sisters had started to instruct me that, for our own safety, it was better not to mention that we were Muslims in public. Perhaps naively, the idea that being a Muslim in India was something that could endanger your life and health shocked me. I had only found my own voice and identity as a Muslim transgender woman by travelling to India. Yet, again and again, India experienced bloody anti-Muslim pogroms.

In 2002, just a few years before I received these grim instructions, an anti-Muslim pogrom occurred in the state of Gujarat, whose Chief Minister at the time was Narendra Modi of the Hindu nationalist BJP party. The anti-Muslim climate in India has become brutal since Modi became Prime Minister in 2014. It is not surprising that in this climate some Indian *hijras* are renouncing their culturally Muslim heritage and their religiously syncretic traditions and trying to become less vulnerable by appealing to Hindu nationalist sentiments. Many Hindu nationalist politicians gladly embrace those *hijras* because it gives them a chance to present their politics as tolerant and inclusive.

It is a tragedy, however, to see how easily traditional transgender communities become a pawn in the games of religious nationalism, losing much of their independent history and their ability to empower social and cultural discourses that connect rather than draw apart different religious identities. We do not have to look to South Asia to understand how much trans and other LGBTQI politics has become a field contested by nationalist political agendas. In 2007, Jasbir Puar used the term 'homonationalism' to refer to the processes by which many governments appear to support the claims of the LGBTQI community in order to justify racism, especially Islamophobia, by claiming that Muslim immigrants are essentially homophobic and transphobic and that Western societies are essentially egalitarian. Many political actors in the West wish to present their own nations as beacons of LGBT rights and safe havens for people who want to express their sexuality freely, exploiting that positive image to distract from negative and discriminatory policies.

In my own work I regularly encounter the impact of homonationalism on our societies. I am often interviewed by journalists in my capacity as a Muslim transgender woman, for example, and I frequently notice that many of these interviews run on the assumption that Muslim immigrants are the main source of transphobia in Germany in particular, or the West in general, and that my life as a transgender woman must be especially difficult because I long for acceptance in a religious community that is, by nature, particularly badly equipped for such acceptance. Interviewing me and other queer Muslim people, therefore, seems to serve the sole purpose of reassuring European mainstream society that a certain fear of the brown Muslim immigrant is justified to at least some extent, if only in the interest of sexual minorities.

But my lived reality has little to do with such assumptions. Granted, transphobia exists in many Muslim circles in Europe.

It was, after all, my experience in a not-so-affirming mosque environment in Germany that led me to my journey to India and Pakistan. Granted also that my own experience is very different from the experience of queer people who have had to flee their Muslim majority home countries because they faced persecution due to their gender identity or sexual orientation. The fact remains, however, that having experienced transphobic and homophobic assaults throughout my life, the vast majority of these painful encounters were with transphobic white Germans. It is the mainstream society around me that I have learned to perceive as the greatest threat to my own safety, not immigrants who are in marginalised positions themselves.

There is a peculiar ignorance of these realities in Western societies these days. We hold an image of our own nations and societies that has little to do with reality but which nevertheless helps us to celebrate our cultural and national identities as inherently superior. This ignorance is always particularly pronounced when it comes to issues of gender and sexuality. The German and pan-European discourse surrounding incidents of sexual assault and pickpocketing at the New Year's Eve celebrations in Cologne and other German cities in 2015/2016 serves as a prime example.

Regrettably, sexual harassment and rape are pretty regular criminal offences when it comes to any mass celebration in Germany, as is pickpocketing. Each year at the Oktoberfest in Munich and the Cologne carnival, numerous assaults are registered by the police, the majority of perpetrators being white Germans. However, in 2015, there was greater scrutiny upon these events because the New Year's Eve celebrations followed a year in which a large number of war refugees from Syria and Afghanistan had been allowed to seek asylum in Germany. When it became known that a number of the suspects in these cases were of North African origin, and some of the suspects asylum seekers, the assaults were quickly blamed on Chancellor Angela

Merkel and other politicians who had welcomed refugees and asylum seekers and refugees were collectively demonised. Right-wing media and politicians rapidly spread the story that German mainstream media and politics had tried to silence any true reporting on these incidents and subsequently a dark narrative about Muslim migrant men conspiring to commit a mass rape of white German women spread across Europe.

A number of feminist analysts expressed their disappointment at the fact that sexual assaults during these events had never drawn as much attention before and that, in general, the European public did not seem to care much about sexual violence committed by white European men. They also drew attention to the sorry fact that, in the stories spread by right-wing populist actors, women were always treated as some kind of commodity. In the end, this story was never about the women involved as such; it was about 'our women', women imagined as belonging exclusively to white European men. Anti-racist activists in Germany also noted that the German police is amongst those institutions in Europe most immune to any criticism of racial profiling—even UN observers had warned that the German police has a strong tendency to select non-white immigrant men as criminal suspects. However, despite these anti-racist, feminist responses, many people across Europe still believe that Cologne witnessed a mass assault of brown Muslim refugee men on native white German women.

These kind of narratives are of a very compelling nature and have contributed to the steep rise in popularity of the AfD, a relatively young right-wing populist party in Germany, and similar right-wing parties all over Europe. The irony of the matter is, however, that none of these right-wing parties has ever shown any genuine interest in protecting the rights of women or of LGBTQI people. In fact, the same parties that routinely accuse Muslim immigrants of homophobic and transphobic violence and of sexist assaults are also trying to introduce anti-LGBTQI and anti-feminist policies into our corpus of laws. In a milder form, the same kind of dissonance can be found amongst more moderate conservative parties in Europe which have made migration the main topic of their election campaigns in recent years. Unfortunately, a number of LGBTQI-identifying people, including a number of LGBTQI-identifying people who come from immigrant Muslim family backgrounds, have joined these efforts to support homonationalist agendas.

I often wonder what purpose LGBTQI-identifying people see in supporting right-wing or conservative policies that will eventually curb their own rights. Their reply would undoubtedly be to ask what I will do when Islamist Muslim immigrants become the majority in our countries and curb my rights, showing only how ever-present the force of right-wing narratives has become. In all affluent Western societies, Muslims are a minority and are likely to remain so in future decades. Even if the horror scenarios of right-wing pundits came true and Muslim migration and reproduction rates doubled—though studies actually suggest that both are slowing down—Muslims would still remain a minority for years to come.[1]

Muslims in the West are not only a numerical minority, but they also face economic, political and educational marginalisation. Apart from that, only the smallest percentage of Muslims in the West follow Islamist ideologies and have any interest in an Islamist state. Many people counted as Muslims in the West are not particularly pious. Separately from this, a large number of Muslims in Germany are Turkish Alevis, some of whom consider themselves to belong to a religion apart from Islam. There is not a single relevant Islamist political force in any parliament in the West, while right-wing populists and increasingly right-leaning conservatives abound. Fear of the proverbial 'creeping shariah' is a pure fantasy in Europe, while fear of right-wing policies that could eventually curb LGBT rights in many Western nations is, unfortunately, based on justified concerns.

The greatest danger that I perceive in homonationalism, however, is its negative influence on global politics. I have alluded elsewhere to the problematic dynamics that arise when some nations insist that the fight for pro-feminist and pro-LGBTQI rights is one which has already been won and firmly established by the West and which now just remains to be exported to the rest of the world by Western political representatives and Western-funded NGOs. The more Western countries culturalise issues such as women's rights and LGBTQI issues, the more despotic regimes in other regions of the world can make reactionary appeals to populist voters by presenting themselves as protectors of traditional family values in opposition. We have seen this happen not only in Muslim majority countries, but also in Russia and amongst Christian evangelical politicians in Africa.

Does this mean that it would be better if Western countries did not try to support LGBTQI rights in other parts of the world? No, not at all. It is important to show solidarity with LGBTQI activists fighting under dire circumstances in countries of the world that lack established legal protections for sexual minorities. It is important that they receive support both from governmental and non-governmental actors from countries where legal protections for sexual minorities have already been established. We can use our privileges to join their fight for justice. But if we really want to affect positive change then we need to stop falling into identitarian traps of 'us vs. them'.

This is not an issue of Islam against Liberal Democracy or the West against the East. It is also not an issue of Russia against Germany or the traditions of Uganda against the traditions of England. I hope that the previous chapters of this book have shown the reader that there is no such thing as a uniform and unchanging culture or tradition. We are all human beings who drink from several sources of wisdom and are nourished by several histories and through that we are able to constantly create new forms of wisdom and nourishment. If in the course of that process we are made to believe that our own desire for safety and happiness is sabotaged by other people's desire for safety and happiness, then we should pause and reflect on how we have come to believe in this lie.

Ultimately, all ostensible cultural oppositions in our world are merely based on power interests. Politicians like Putin and Trump, for example, regularly talk about traditional values but observation shows that they do not live by these values at all. Right-wing and conservative rhetoric surrounding migration leads us to believe that immigrants have come to 'our countries' to steal what rightfully only belongs to us, while the people who promulgate these narratives make sure that, via tax exemptions and an increasingly deregulated global market, we are robbed of better lives every single day. Increasingly militarised borders affect the most vulnerable, who are often fleeing from circumstances that our nations have created, while regulations go unenforced when it comes to big corporations exploiting millions of people.

In the midst of all this, we have forgotten to strive for the things that would really give us all safety and happiness. We have probably all learned at some point that this planet has enough resources to feed every single hungry mouth in this world while still retaining a surplus. But, somehow, we are afraid of the idealist politics which asks to make this vision a reality. Instead we prefer to be afraid of the 'other', whether that other is Muslim or Hindu, 'Eastern' or 'Western'. We cling to that fear because it gives us a convenient excuse not to question the political, social and economic reality that we live in.

10

SEX AND THE COSMOPOLIS

IT HAS BEEN MORE than two decades now that I have been connected to a transgender/*khwajasara*/*hijra* network spanning not only several nations of South Asia, but also Europe, South Africa, North America and, in fact, the whole globe. It may at first glance seem that my own life has been a uniquely global experience in this network, but that's not the case. I was joined by many others on my journey. At the beginning of this book, I spoke of how my path was shaped by the emergence of the internet in the 1990s and the new chances to connect with people globally that it brought. It was through connections to other queer Muslims worldwide, to other transgender women in the US and to the South Asian LGBT community that my own horizons expanded. But this was not just my experience; it was our collective experience. And soon after, these virtual encounters translated into journeys in the real world.

It was around the time of my initial travels to India that others had started to organise the first international queer Muslim retreats and conferences. And it only took a few years more for a global discussion on trans rights, on the one hand, and a fascination with traditional South Asian third-gender communities, on the other, to lead to the first of several prominent transgender, *khwajasara* and *hijra* activists being invited to these and other international events. This has also caused new frictions in the community because not everybody gets regularly invited abroad; not everybody gets to stay in fancy hotels in Amsterdam, Cape Town or Bangkok; and not everybody gets the attention of such an international audience. There is a vast world of traditional *hijra deras* which will never have any connection with such events. But then there are the few prominent names from India and Pakistan who have become part of a group of international *khwajasara/hijra* 'jet-setters'. And many more who hope to become a part of that group one day.

One could be tempted to say that this is an entirely new situation for traditional communities such as the *khwajasaras*. At several points in this book, I've described the community as closed and partly secretive, and the word 'traditional' in itself often invokes ideas of a preserved, isolated conservativism in our minds. But 'tradition' never emerges out of the blue and it is always sustained by other influences. In that sense, I should caution the reader not to take my characterisation of a 'closed' community too literally. What has been hidden and isolated from the world beyond has always been determined by specific historical circumstances and dependent on what was needed for survival. But, of course, the community always existed as a part of a wider society and a wider global world as well.

In general, the dominant social discourse in many Western societies still seems to think of the world as arbitrarily divided into an 'East' and a 'West', with the 'West' and all its achievements of modernity and enlightenment now ushering in a completely new age of globalisation. That this is a very twisted image of reality should be apparent to anyone who has studied global history. Global interconnections are nothing new. Baltic amber and Afghan lapis lazuli have been found in the tomb of the ancient Egyptian Pharaoh Tutankhamen (died c. 1323 BCE). These precious substances did not arrive there by themselves, of course. We have to picture vast networks of people engaging with each other to connect Northern Europe with Egypt and Afghanistan more than 3,000 years ago. And contact between peoples always means contact between cultures, worldviews and ideas—including ideas on gender and sexuality.

During my stay in the *dera* in Delhi our grandmother guru often told me that once there had been a time when the *hijra* community had existed 'from Spain to China'. She was quite convinced of that, though she was never able to tell me much more about that early global history. I imagine that her words reflect an echo of knowledge about the spread of Islam in its early centuries. Maybe there is also an echo of the famous line from the South Asian Muslim philosopher and writer Muhammad Iqbal's poem *Tarana-e-Milli*, in which he states: 'China is ours, Arabia is ours, India is ours. We are Muslim and the whole world is ours.' But since our grandmother guru saw herself as a direct heir to a line of royal eunuchs, she may have been correct in identifying the history of her community with a global history of Islamicate courtly culture. Or was her memory going back to times even before that? Maybe to the times of Bagoas, the beautiful Persian eunuch lover of Alexander the Great who accompanied him on many of his journeys and battles between Macedonia, India, North Africa and Central Asia. Or perhaps even longer ago.

The *hijra/khwajasara* community has, as such, a global origin mythology as well. And this mythology represents an awareness of the fact that this community has always been connected to the world. It has been shaped by it and, in turn, has also played a part in shaping it.

I have already mentioned the strange similarities between the cult of the goddess Bahuchara Mata, which, particularly in Gujarat, Mumbai and in some parts of South India, is closely associated with the *hijra* community, and the antique Greco-Roman mystery cult of the Anatolian goddess Kybele and her companion Attis. What happened here? Are these just coincidences? Or maybe they represent a cultural transfer during the Hellenistic age, when Greco-Iranian dynasties were ruling from Anatolia and Egypt to Northern India? Or maybe this is something brought to Gujarat by sailors? We know, after all, that Gujarat once had flourishing trade with the Roman Empire. Or does this all harken back to even more ancient times, to my grandmother guru's mythical era when 'the *hijra* community existed from Spain to China'?

We also learn from the work of Jessica Hinchy, which I referred to in Chapter 3, that the eunuch societies and families in the Muslim courts of South Asia practised their own version of a globalised cosmopolitan culture. Historian Richard M. Eaton (see also Chapter 7) also notes that during the Persianate Age (approximately 1000 to 1800 CE), India constantly received waves of migration from West and Central Asia, while also engaging in trade with the wider world. The ethos in the courts of this era has been labelled the 'Bengal-to-Balkan-complex' by the late scholar Shahab Ahmed in his book *What is Islam? The Importance of Being Islamic.*[1] In this vast region spanning from south-eastern Europe to South Asia, a certain tradition of learning was encouraged that often began with the study of the Quran and the sayings of the Prophet, and continued with both Greek philosophy and the works of Persian poets such as Sa'adi and Hafiz. Hinchy explains that precisely this kind of education was received when one was inducted into the courtly eunuch family.

The eunuchs who were educated in this way came from all over the world and had very different backgrounds. Many of them were indeed young men who were enslaved and forcibly castrated on faraway shores. In the early years of India's Persianate Age, many of these would have come from Eastern Europe, Central Asia or the Caucasus. Later, many were abducted from Africa. But, as already mentioned, many 'born eunuchs' were among them, most of whom would have been of local South Asian origin. The make-up of the courtly eunuch societies was as such no less international than that of modern *khwajasara* and *hijra* communities, where, in addition to Indians and Pakistanis, we will find Bangladeshis, Nepalis, Afghans and the occasional European too.

But what do these cosmopolitan pasts have to do with the globalisation of the community today?

Fortunately, nowadays we have a far greater understanding of how much the global modern world has been shaped by earlier forms of globalisation, and that in those globalisations the West was only rarely the dominant actor. It hardly even existed as a uniform 'West'. We still do not often realise how much our modern world and its ideas and concepts have been shaped not only by Europe but also by the Islamic world and the Global South's engagement with Europe. In his 2007 text 'There Never was a West', the late anthropologist David Graeber, for example, pointed out that there is no direct thread linking ancient Athens to twenty-first-century democracy, and that modern democracy may actually owe much more to mixed-race international pirate polities in the Mediterranean, the Caribbean and on the North American coast.

Graeber also notes that 'Opposition to European expansion in much of the world, even quite early on, appears to have been carried out in the name of "Western values" that the Europeans in question did not yet even have.'[2] In that context, he cites the case of the sixteenth-century Indian Muslim scholar Zayn al-Din Malabari, who described fending off the invading Portuguese as being a defence of tolerance and pluralism. In fact, in a period in which the political and territorial expansion of European powers such as the Spanish or the Portuguese was inevitably also connected to a spread of repressive religious institutions such as the Inquisition, South Asian Muslim polities have often referred to the idealised principle that 'a state can be sustained with justice without religion, but it cannot be sustained with religion without justice' (in Muslim tradition variously attributed to the Prophet himself or to Imam 'Ali or other important figures). Of course, in Muslim societies too the reality was often far from the ideal. But the important point is that modern conceptions of freedom, justice and democracy are not merely European inventions, but emerged globally and had multiple roots.

In the nineteenth century, the age of developing modern cosmopolitanism, political changes swiftly followed the emergence of new conceptions of freedom, justice and democracy. But here too it is wrong to assume, as is too often done, that these political transformations were simply a result of an 'export of European values', and that colonial subjects merely learned about their human rights from their overlords and then rebelled. Often it was the new awareness of a wider and far more plural and diverse world that made European thinkers first explore issues such as universal human rights. And they often came late to such realisations, which had already been discussed by figures such as the thirteenth-century Persian poet Sa'adi: 'Human beings are members of a whole/In creation of one essence and soul/If one member is afflicted with pain/Other members uneasy will remain/If you have no sympathy for human pain/The name of human you cannot retain.'[3] This in itself was a poem originally based on a *hadith* of the Prophet Muhammad (p.b.u.h.) and a saying of Imam 'Ali.

When the spirit of revolution eventually erupted, it erupted globally. The Haitian Revolution, of 1791–1804, for example, took place contemporaneously with the French Revolution. And the mid-1800s saw the almost simultaneous outbreak of revolutionary uprisings both in several European countries and in India. Unbeknownst to many, individuals from South Asia played an important role in political developments in Europe. Abbé Faria, a Goan Catholic Brahmin born in Candolim, for example, travelled to Europe and took part both in a conspiracy against the King of Portugal and in the French Revolution, before becoming Professor of Philosophy at the University of France in Nîmes in 1811 and advancing the scientific study of hypnotism and psychology. Writer Alexandre Dumas, himself a child of a global world, named a character in his *The Count of Monte Cristo* after Faria. There was also Quint Ondaatje, a

Sri Lankan Burgher of Tamil origin. The mixed-heritage Ondaatje played a formative role in the founding of the Batavian Republic in The Netherlands, and is remembered as a champion of Dutch democracy and as someone who put a great emphasis on 'freedom of speech', now thought of as a quintessentially 'Dutch' idea.

Where do sex and gender feature in all of this? As natural components of all human existence, we must conceive of them as implicitly present in all these processes as well. The revolutionaries of this world all had ideas on sex and gender. And quite often they came to the fore. The nineteenth century saw a rise in awareness and concern for women's rights, and the question of women's 'suffrage' increasingly became a question of global politics. It also saw the decriminalisation of homosexuality under the French Napoleonic Code and in the new laws of the Tanzimat era under the Ottoman Empire.

More importantly, however, we need to understand that new global connections and intersections between societies in the nineteenth century also affected sexual minorities living within them. And these sexual minorities also played a role (unfortunately not too well documented) in these connections and intersections. We can see glimpses of that role, for example, in the secret language of nineteenth-century British gay and trans people, Polari. Just as *hijras* and *khwajasaras* in South Asia today have their own secret argot, *farsi*, in which they can communicate in ways inaccessible to others, British queer people once used to have such language too. Polari is a unique mix of slang, Yiddish words and Romani idioms, which in itself testifies to the subaltern cosmopolitanism within which it emerged.

But a large part of its vocabulary (words such as *'bona'* for good, or *'fantabulosa'*) seem to derive from Mediterranean Romance languages. Some scholars have suggested that the most likely candidate for this origin language would be the

Mediterranean Lingua Franca, or *Sabir*, a pidgin language once spoken in harbours and among pirates all across the Mediterranean and beyond. The transfer of vocabulary from a pidgin language of sailors and pirates to the secret argot of gay and trans people should not surprise any scholar of queer histories: the waterfront of the harbour cities of Western and Western-ruled societies was throughout the nineteenth and early twentieth century one of the main locations in which marginalised queer communities could feel at home. It was the site of both free and paid sexual and romantic encounters with 'men of the sea', and a space to feel at least partially liberated of social and political censorship.

The Global South also comes into contact with the West at those waterfronts. This happens quite obviously in the big harbour towns of South Asia, such as colonial Calcutta (Kolkata) and Bombay (Mumbai). But it also occurs on European and North American shores. Brazilian queer historian Luiz Mott documents the sixteenth-century story of Vitoria, a Black person born in Benin, West Africa, who would perhaps be recognised today as a transgender woman or an otherwise transfeminine person. She dressed as a woman and engaged in sex work on the riverbanks of Lisbon. We only know her story because she was eventually arrested by the Inquisition, which documented her case. But it is not unimaginable that she was just one of many queer people from Africa, and possibly also from other parts of the colonial Portuguese world such as India, who ended up in Europe and became part of the 'waterfront scene' there.

If such connections were already possible in the sixteenth century, they had certainly developed much further by the nineteenth and early twentieth century. Partly due to the opening of the Suez Canal in 1869, these greater connectivities would lead to a much stronger presence of individuals from South Asia and the Muslim world in the harbour cities of the West. Here as well we unfortunately often face a lack of documentation, but glimpses of a lived reality can be seen in the few sources we have. Hugh Ryan, author of *When Brooklyn was Queer*, told me that Indian and Middle Eastern sailors occasionally came up in the materials he sifted through during his research. Ryan explained: 'Hamilton Easter Field, who ran an arts salon on the waterfront in the early 1900s, had some contact with a number of different people from India and the Middle East. Truman Capote writes about many different kinds of sailors in *A House on the Heights* though, and specifically calls out East Indian and Senegalese sailors.'

Curiously, the early 1900s were also the time when early pioneers of Islam in New York City started to involve seafaring workers into their community activities. As Rasul Miller writes in his article 'The Black American Sufi: A History',[4] the Grenadan sufi leader Shaykh Daoud Ahmed Faisal and his Bermudan wife Khadijah, who founded a mosque in Brooklyn in 1939, were especially dedicated to such efforts. Although we are speaking about two largely disconnected areas of research. It is not difficult to imagine a Bengali Muslim sailor visiting the mosque and sufi gatherings of Shaykh Daoud on the one hand, and having intimate relationships with a local transfeminine person on the other. And he would have not considered these two parts of his life more in conflict with each other in Brooklyn than he would have in India, where such interactions could likewise have been a very normal and regular part of his life. In that way, religious spaces and spaces of queer sexuality would overlap again and again, in Kolkata, in Bombay and in Brooklyn.

At the same time, Europe's colonial encounter with the world also made Europeans more aware of the fact that sexuality and gender were not thought of in the same way everywhere. This could result in ugly Orientalist stereotypes that still haunt us today, such as that about the barbarous and licentious Muslim man who is at the same time sexually repressed and out of control. But it also led some Europeans to think more inquisitively about sexuality and gender. It was, in fact, the European encounter with the sexualities and gender identities of the Global South that eventually gave birth to the conceptions of sexual identity, orientation and freedom that we are so familiar with today.

A crucial role in this process was played by Magnus Hirschfeld, the German-Jewish sexologist discussed in Chapter 3. Hirschfeld is today often celebrated as a hero of the early LGBTQI movement, even though his ideas and practices were sometimes problematic. In essence, Hirschfeld's concepts of sexuality and health were motivated by a very modern desire for social engineering. But he was also one of the first people who consciously used his scientific inquiry to defend the rights of sexual minorities. He was one of the first Western scholars to come up with the idea of immutable sexual identities and orientations that people are born with and that they cannot change. And in that he was strongly influenced by anthropological discoveries of the time, including reports about homosexuality occurring in virtually all human societies, with varying degrees of acceptance, and ideas of 'third genders' in several societies, such as in South Asia. In 1931, Hirschfeld came to visit India, where he met Jawaharlal Nehru and voiced his support for Indian independence.

Hirschfeld died in 1935 and the German Nazi regime tried its best to erase his legacy. But it is well known and in subsequent decades it was taken up in particular by US sexologists, inspiring a lot of the American liberation discourse on sexuality and gender that still defines the LGBTQI movement today. As discussed in Chapter 3, one of his closest associates, Hugo Hamid Marcus, an openly homosexual convert to Islam, was a vocal advocate for the rights of sexual minorities.

What we see here is that the histories of a modern global Islam and of a modern global LGBTQI movement are not isolated from each other. Whether it is in Indian and Arab sailors at the Brooklyn waterfront or whether it is in people such as Hugo Hamid Marcus, they intersected and entwined. And the examples that I have provided here are only among the few that current research can document. I am certain that with a more dedicated quest one would be able to unearth many other examples of such seemingly surprising relationships.

But since these intersections in the early twentieth century, global Islam has followed many of its own twists and turns, some of which I have spoken about in Chapters 4, 5 and 9. The rise of essentialising fundamentalist movements in Islam is a part of globalisation and cosmopolitanisation as well, of course, just as is the rise of nationalism. The global LGBTQI movement has also followed its own winding and complicated route. It has developed conceptions derived from the thoughts of Hirschfeld, while also advancing ideas much less grounded in historical and anthropological research.

There is a significant division between how LGBTQI people understood their gender and their sexuality at the beginning of the twentieth century and how they did at the end of the same century. In Chapter 3, I mentioned that Hirschfeld had come to understand the several forms of homosexuality and various gender identities as constituting some kind of 'third gender'. In Chapter 7, I also spoke about how in the early twentieth century in urban settings of the West, gay and trans identities did indeed exist much more in a fluid continuum, while at the same time the desired sexual and romantic partner of both gay men and trans-feminine people would often have been a straight heterosexual man, just as is today the case for many *khwajasaras* and *hijras*.

These kind of notions changed completely over the course of the twentieth century, and when we look at the attitudes towards sex and gender of a lot of queer people in our own societies, we often find them at least as strange and as unintelligible as attitudes in other societies and cultures. That process also created conflict and ruptures within urban LGBTQI communities in the West. Sylvia Rivera (1951–2002), the American LGBTQI rights campaigner, emblematically stood at the crossroads of this process. Looking back on her life, she is often remembered as a transgender activist, but she herself actually rejected the word transgender throughout her life, instead referring to herself as a 'gay transvestite' or a 'street queen', while using female pronouns, presenting as female and expressing a feminine identity. Her self-identification often aggravated the middle-class gay community of her time, which thought that any identification with femininity or drag could potentially damage the progress of gay rights. Likewise, today it often seems anathema to how most transgender activists want to be seen and want to see themselves. Both the gay and the transgender community sometimes celebrate her as an early hero, but it is not rare to hear LGBT people today say that Rivera 'simply didn't understand herself properly', that she didn't 'do' gender and sexuality in the right way. We find here the same kind of attitude with which the contemporary global LGBT movement often views traditional and local sexualities and gender identities.

In fact, Sylvia Rivera just represented an alternative way of understanding sexuality and gender in a globalising world, one that was as much informed by the previous histories of queer New York as by her Puerto Rican and Venezuelan family origins—a way of expressing sexuality that many others used to share, but which was subsequently marginalised. First, queer working-class and immigrant communities in the urban West were 'mainstreamed' to practise sexuality and gender 'properly'. Then that project was extended to the wider post-colonial world.

But many ways of understanding sexuality and gender still resist this mainstreaming, and have managed to make it onto the global stage. While international 'rainbow' organisations and NGOs may be the most visible examples of global sexuality and gender in our age, there are other processes of cosmopolitanisation at work too. Just as the stories of African trans women in Portugal or queer sailors and their lovers in Kolkata, Bombay and Brooklyn have only rarely been recorded, these processes of cosmopolitanisation are also little acknowledged today. But this does not make them any less important for our future ideas on these topics.

Hijra and *khwajasara* activists from South Asia who become jet-setters (and trend-setters) at conferences in Amsterdam and Cape Town, and a German Muslim trans woman searching for her identity in India and Pakistan, are but two images from our connected queer worlds today. There are many more *khwajasaras* who arrived as refugees in the EU or the UK and who continue to live aspects of traditional *khwajasara* life in cities such as Frankfurt or Berlin, while at the same time engaging with local gay and trans communities and fighting against the traumatising system of immigration bureaucracy. They are invited to conferences or to give talks far less frequently, and their voices are rarely heard. They also may not want to publish a book. But they do have an impact both on the societies in which they were born and the societies in which they arrive.

It is, at this point, important to note that cosmopolitanisation and globalisation are also violent processes. In the past, the eunuch societies in Muslim courts were shaped by wars, displacement and enslavement. Today, war, but also impoverishment, are major causes of migration. And this impoverishment is tied to the same neoliberal capitalist system that fuels much of the global discourse on gender and sexuality today. For a lot of LGBTQI people from Muslim majority and other countries of the Global South, another reason for migration is to escape legal systems that criminalise their identities and their romantic and sexual relationships. Even where there has been recent progress on trans rights, and where trans people have something of a legally recognised status, such as in Iran or Pakistan, there is still a lot of insecurity, instability and arbitrariness in legal matters. This, just as much as political corruption, weighs heavily on many LGBTQI people, leading them to hope that life elsewhere may be easier.

These hopes are sometimes fuelled by illusions generated by the world of LGBT jet-setters and NGOs. I've found that in a lot of Muslim majority societies, many LGBT people think that if only they could come out and build their lives according to the demands of a globalised Western LGBTQI model, they would eventually end up with happy long-term relationships that are fully acknowledged by friends and family, and with a fancy rainbow-striped bungalow by the beach. It fits the fantasy of global gay culture. I have already mentioned in Chapter 7 that the reality unfortunately looks very different even for many LGBT people born and raised in the West, and that the project of sexual liberation has in fact made many things painful and traumatic, particularly for transgender women.

But what is even more painful is that people of course do not automatically become happy and free just by changing the legal framework that they must survive. They may just as easily find themselves caught up in another brutal system of laws. I have witnessed the shattered illusions of asylum seekers who came to the West in the hope of a liberated life. Their journey did indeed grant them an important freedom from legal persecution and from the burden of constantly having to hide socially. But their lives also did not turn out to be the happy fairy-tales that they had imagined. They have struggled consistently with structural discrimination and racism, and often discover that finding love is, ironically, much more difficult for them in the 'free' West than it was in their criminalising and socially repressive home countries.

So, what would have been the better solution for them? Staying in their countries of origin and dealing with police raids and with intolerant family members who may wish to do them harm? Certainly not. That is not an option either. But they live in a world that is structured in such a way that a working-class queer person from a Muslim majority country would always find themselves under some form of oppression, no matter where they are.

I therefore think that if we really want to see progress and equality for LGBTQI people in this constantly globalising world, we need a better focus on issues of practical social justice. And that also has to mean that we must give up ideological illusions and promises. These promises are not real. They are mythology. They haven't held true for the vast majority of LGBTQI people in the West and even less will they hold true for LGBTQI people in Muslim majority countries or elsewhere in the Global South.

In a world in which we deal with a multiplicity of cultural ideas on sexuality and gender, what is needed instead is that we raise the demand for tangible rights. People may have different thoughts and feelings on the question of coming out or on how precisely to define their gender. There can be cultural variation here. But even laying aside ideas of cultural or ideological belonging, every human being wants to be free of fear and free of legal and social discrimination.

An example of the extent to which ideological mythology is restricting serious efforts to move towards a better world for us all is the ludicrous amount of effort that many LGBTQI organisations and activists today put into spreading the idea that homosexuality is a sexual orientation that people are born with. But the truth is that there is no objective science on this issue. One can argue for both sides and find scientists and scientific models supporting you either way. But the more pressing question in that context is: What if it is not something we are born with? What if we cannot prove it is? Just imagine that.

Would that then mean that people who engage in homosexual activity (no matter how they identify or define themselves) deserve to be killed for it, or otherwise criminalised and punished? Of course not. Therefore, issues of human rights should never be mixed up with ideological imaginings and mythologies around sexuality and gender. Let us instead agree that people should not be punished for homosexual activities. Let us agree that people should not be discriminated against for being transgender. What precise conceptions we may or may not share on 'how to do sexuality properly' or 'how to do gender properly' should be left out of these discussions. They are of no consequence here. Only then can we have a truly global discourse on LGBTQI rights.

CONCLUSION

PAST, PRESENT AND FUTURE

IN THIS BOOK I have been looking back at my personal history, beginning from the story of a genderqueer Muslim kid in a small town in rural Germany and evolving into a journey of faith, identity and self-discovery, spanning Europe and South Asia. But in the course of this exploration, it's also become obvious that I've always had an obsession with broader histories, and how I fit into them—the history of our modern conceptions of sexuality and gender; the history of Islam; and the history of South Asia.

I simply cannot conceive of telling my own story without starting with my family's roots and backgrounds; I feel indebted to those origins. And not only for the personal aspects—I always feel that my story would be incomplete without explaining something of the stirrings of history that eventually made it possible for me to be born at the time and in the place I was. I have mentioned how, from an early age, I've dived intellectually into the histories of Egypt, China and eventually India. I was always searching for answers to my own immediate and present problems by looking to the past. People in my life will attest to the fact that this is still a constant occupation for me. Probably not a single day passes without me reading, writing, talking about history—whether it be my personal history, my family history or the history of our world.

Not everybody will agree with me on the necessity of this. I have mentioned already that my father, in particular, was always much more a man of the present, and the future. Family history never concerned him as much as it did me. I often encounter a similar attitude in wider society. When I returned from my first stay with a *hijra* community in India, I was astonished to find that not everybody in the trans community, for example, was interested in the history and customs of a centuries-old South Asian third-gender community. I returned to Germany excited and empowered, wanting to share this with other transgender people. But when I told them about my experiences and discoveries, I was often greeted with an uninterested shrug. 'What relevance does this have to our lives?', seemed to be the most common response to my discoveries.

Granted, the organised trans community in Germany at that time mostly consisted of white, middle-class people who did not share my specific concerns with faith and identity. Things changed considerably in the following years. More and more young people of Muslim faith or family background, and more and more young people of colour, entered spaces in German mainstream society that they had previously been excluded from, and they have made their voices and demands heard. In the course of this development, greater numbers of queer and trans Muslims and people of colour came to the fore to speak about their own specific intersectional struggles. In that context there emerged a place for my story as well.

Young queer Muslims in particular became interested in my experience, and I was increasingly invited by them to give talks and workshops on Muslim trans histories and Muslim trans identities. I am very thankful that these young people think that my story may offer them empowerment and inspiration, even more so since many of their struggles are quite different from my own. I do not have to combat racism every day in the same way that many of them have to. And I never had to fight parents or other overbearing family members who thought that they knew better about Islam than I did. It makes me happy that my own journey sometimes helps others, facing infinitely tougher struggles, to walk a few steps with their head higher in the air.

Every now and then during my talks and workshops, however, I do encounter people who seem to think that all of my talk about histories and ancient traditions is not of much use to them. I have heard, a few times, from certain young queer Muslims that they consider all of these old stories rather pointless when confronted with the homophobia and transphobia in their own families and communities, or in their countries of origin. For some of these young people, the present looks very threatening and dark; dreaming of a distant past that may or may not have been better just looks like escapism, something that would divert them from the actual fight they need to fight. I can only accept their truth; I haven't walked in their shoes. I am in no position to tell them what is going to help them.

What does frustrate me is that, of those I've encountered who seem to think that the Muslim past has nothing to offer to us, most *haven't* been young Muslim LGBTQI people; rather, this attitude comes more from people who see themselves as defenders of mainstream Western society's sublime status, and as 'objective' critics of Islam. On more than one occasion, I have been harshly critiqued by people who insisted that my work was nothing but an Orientalist romanticisation and glorification of the past, serving only to make people ignore the real crisis that Islam is experiencing today—to these people, my narrative sweeps that current crisis of patriarchal chauvinism, transphobia and homophobia under some kind of nostalgic 'Arabian Nights' carpet.

To this accusation, my answer will always be that very few people—myself included—would claim that the Muslim past was a paradise on Earth. I have emphasised in previous chapters that every human society creates boundaries and restrictions that are experienced by some as oppressive, and that every human culture gives birth to monsters. But I believe just as strongly that every human culture carries positive potential as well, and that there is something that we can learn by properly analysing the origins and formative influences of cultural practices.

I also think that, even though no society on Earth has ever been a paradise, and even though it is certainly true that Muslim history was never happy and free for everybody, it is objectively verifiable that many past Muslim societies offered queer people a lot more freedom of expression than has been the case since colonial times; it would be foolish of us not to ask whether our histories could not also offer us pathways to better futures, or at least a way to avoid past mistakes. I believe very strongly in the idea once verbalised so eloquently by George Santayana: 'Those who cannot remember the past are condemned to repeat it.' We have, in a way, our own Muslim version of that principle in the verses of the Quran, about the ruins and remains of previous nations: 'And indeed, you pass by them in the morning, and at night. So will you not reflect on them?' (Surah 37, Ayaat 137–138).

When I grew up in a small town in Germany, I had many reasons not to be delighted about the world I was living in. Nevertheless, this was a world that still believed very strongly in progress. I witnessed the end of the Cold War and the fall of a Stalinist dictatorship in one part of my home country. German reunification gave us a strong sense of a future that could only be better than the present. At roughly the same time, other developments happened all over the world that were perceived by many as positive. In South Asia, for example, the year 1988 saw the sudden death of Pakistan's military dictator Zia-ul-Haq, and new hopes were raised, both for a democratic Pakistan and for peace on the subcontinent. In 1992, political scientist Francis Fukuyama promised us an 'End of History' that would eventually manifest in a worldwide spread of liberal democracy. There was also increased talk of gay and trans rights in the media, and many young queer people of my age probably thought we could take it for granted that 'things will get better'.

This optimism of the late 1980s and early 1990s has now largely been shattered; in a strange way, I often feel incredibly sorry for the young people who have grown up since, who have never known this kind of naive conviction of a better future. While I am writing this, the consensus among people I know in the US, the UK, Germany, Pakistan, India and elsewhere seems to be that 2020 was the worst year everybody had ever experienced. The ongoing Covid-19 pandemic has brought many of us to the limits of both physical and emotional patience; has severely harmed the economies of many nations; and has negatively affected many poor and marginalised queer and trans communities, among them the South Asian *hijra* and *khwajasara* community.

Covid may eventually turn out to be rather a small issue compared to the other global problems whose full impact still awaits us. Right before the start of the pandemic, the political topic discussed most widely across the world was impending climate breakdown. Even though some people seem to be in denial of this reality, the vast majority of scientific experts have presented us with depressing prognoses and predictions that seem to promise nothing less than eventual doom. Rich and affluent nations of Europe and the Global North may survive this promised catastrophe to some extent, but it is very clear that many other nations will not. It is also clear that the social injustices of our world will only be exacerbated in that process. We can already see that this will disproportionately affect large parts of the Muslim world and South Asian society, while the leaders of these countries act as though they are in complete ignorance of this reality. The glaciers of the Himalaya mountains, the main source of water for the rivers of Pakistan, India, Nepal and Bangladesh, are already disappearing with worrying speed, while the desert of the Middle East and North Africa region is expanding more and more.

Some people will say that, at such a moment of impending global crisis, we should not waste our attention on issues such as gender and sexuality. But, as always in moments of economic, social and political crisis, we can expect that these pressures will lead tensions to arise surrounding minorities, with issues such as gender and sexuality becoming political battlegrounds. It will therefore be of utmost importance in future years of increasing global insecurity to keep an eye on queer, trans and other LGBTQI people in South Asia and the Muslim world; to take efforts to make sure that their rights will soon reach a status that guarantees them full legal protection. We can also expect—and indeed already begin to see—that, in times of crisis, increasingly myopic religious-extremist and nationalist ideologies gain ground. These currents will always strengthen oppressive social structures and restrict the freedom of women, ethnic and religious minorities and LGBTQI people.

Societies in the Global North are as badly equipped for sailing through the storms of looming crisis as majority Muslim and South Asian societies. They may have a stronger foundation for economic survival but the rise of right-wing populism has prevented these societies from developing any sustainable strategies for the future. In the US, the UK and continental Europe, they have made sure that anxieties about social change have been channelled into issues of immigration and fear of Muslims. Even moderate politicians have adopted a discourse that speaks of a 'flood' of refugees when, as a percentage of the entire population of these affluent nations, one can only truly speak of a trickle; they speak of a 'crisis' that has actually never been a crisis (Covid-19 and climate change should teach us what a real crisis looks like). At the same time as this hostility to the 'other' has grown, almost all Global North societies have continued to suffer from demographic ageing, suggesting that they will not be able to survive economically without increased immigration; and the global threat of climate change means that this increased immigration will certainly happen.

CONCLUSION

We may build higher walls and militarise our borders, but still this can't be escaped. As these irreconcilable realities collide, we will witness increasingly vicious human rights abuses at the outer fringes, abuses we will all finance through taxes and support through apathy. That, again, will hit marginalised people more than anybody else. At the same time, the Global North will probably continue to celebrate its societies as beacons of human rights, feminism and sexual and gender freedom. But the West's time may be up.

Historically, this interval of Global North dominance has been not much more than a curiosity. Western and Northern Europe has, for the larger part of human history, been a civilisational backwater: most social and cultural progress has happened in Asia and Africa, and only those parts of Europe closest to Africa and Asia (Greece and Italy, for example) have been included in that orbit of civilisation. Today, the countries of the Arabian Peninsula and the Persian Gulf often lack democracy and freedom, but these countries have now become serious players in geopolitics and the global economy. I wonder how many of the English people afraid of poor Arab and Muslim immigrants and their 'foreign culture' know or care that, as of 2020, one of the biggest property tycoons in London is the president of the United Arab Emirates, Sheikh Khalifa bin Zayed Al-Nahyan. At the same time, many Global South regimes that previously looked to the West as a guarantor of power and stability are now striking deals with China instead. In other words, the days when the West made the rules for the rest of the planet are already counted. That in itself should make us more willing to engage constructively with non-Western ideas of gender and sexuality, because Western culture may not be the gold standard for much longer.

Many of my readers may be gripped by an even stronger fear of change than the Islamophobes and transphobes, and that fear may tempt some of them to perceive non-Western societies as even more threatening and hostile than before. But I would like to remind these readers that, throughout its history, humanity has always found its way. And it has often been the more affluent and dominant societies that eventually became guarantors of freedom; the Muslim world was at its most tolerant during those days when it was globally most influential. So, eventually, a change in power balances might also open up new doors to new progress. And, in any case, neither nations nor cultures have ever remained static entities. In the new world born of the pandemic and the climate crisis, we may also see new possibilities. Instead of remaining stuck in a tiring opposition of East and West, Occident and Islam, we may eventually end up with hybrid spiritual and cultural identities such as the one dreamed up by the science-fiction writer Frank Herbert, who imagined in *Dune* (1965) a distant future in which people would adhere to religions such as Buddislam, Mahayana Christianity and Zensunni Catholicism.

I do not want my predictions to eventually become as redundant as Fukuyama's *End of History*. But looking back at human history, I can say with some conviction that we will probably neither see Paradise nor Hell on Earth any time soon. What we will see is a lot of change. And we will think about a lot of things—gender and sexuality included—in ways that we would never have expected. That is something to be excited about.

The year 2020 was most definitely not the worst year in human history. I can say that with some conviction, thanks to looking at the past. People who experienced the Mongol conquests or the Black Death, or who survived the colonial genocide of the Spanish in what was to become Latin America, would find such a notion absurd, as would those who lived through World War I, World War II and the Holocaust. But many of us have been confronted with fears in these times with which we have never been confronted before. And we cannot believe as naively in progress anymore as we did a few decades ago.

CONCLUSION

The Indian writer Amitav Ghosh addressed this less optimistic spirit of our times during a 2019 discussion at the Library of Congress National Book Festival in Washington, DC. He noted that he feels the religious perspective on history may be a much better way to face our current world than the narrative of progress that still forms the basis for so much Western and Western-influenced political thought and action. Religions, after all, often expect that things will get worse. Both Christians and Muslims expect the rise of the Antichrist and increasing catastrophes before the advent of the Saviour and the Last Judgment. Buddhism and Hinduism speak of a 'Dark Age' or an 'Age of Decline' awaiting us before the arrival of the Maitreya Buddha or the last avatar of Lord Vishnu. Ghosh notes that people who believe in such ideas may actually be much better prepared to act responsibly in a world in crisis than people who place their faith in science and technology, and always take progress for granted. In that sense, we may also embrace our apocalyptic fears as something that may motivate us to make actual positive change.

The religious vision, of course, never *ends* with doom and terror. Naturally, some Muslims (and many Christians) believe that the future arrival of the Saviour will elevate their own specific identities, and their own specific truths. But there is actually a delightfully subversive element in many Muslim traditions surrounding the arrival of the Saviour. The medieval Sunni mystic Ibn 'Arabi once mentioned in his *Futuhat* that the Mahdi will not rule as the orthodox Muslim scholars expect him to rule, and the religious scholars will actually be in opposition to him. And one of the Shi'a Imams said: 'The descendants of the Prophet will desert the Mahdi, and the polytheist worshippers of the sun and moon will come to his aid.' In the end, Paradise itself may not very much abide by the rules of people who always thought of themselves as destined for it. Who may or may not be destined for Paradise or for Hell is contested in Muslim tradition, as is the question of whether Hell will be eternal, or whether its sufferings will be terminated by God at some point. In a narration from the first Shi'a Imam 'Ali ibn Abi Talib, peace be upon him, and also found in the Sunni scripture Sahih Tirmidhi, it is said that there will be a marketplace in Paradise where everybody can change into whatever they want to change into whenever they want. And the Imam emphasises, 'no matter whether that may be a male or female form'. For me, there is something essentially 'queer' about such religious visions of the future.

Eventually, when the big drama of the Last Judgment has passed, and everybody has been settled comfortably or uncomfortably in Paradise or Hell, God may initiate the creation of a new universe. In a narration from one of the later Shi'a Imams, Muhammad al-Baqir, peace be upon him, it is said: 'And God will create a new creation, without male and female, who will worship Him and His oneness.'

To the believer, and maybe the non-believer as well, these and other narrations may serve as a reminder that none of our contested identities are as essential as we often think they are. They are a great witness to the idea I have invoked above, the idea that humankind always finds its way. Even in the middle of religious and cultural traditions that at first sight may seem dogmatic and inflexible, we can find a spirit of creativity and diversity, and hopes for a future in which we think differently. Accessing this spirit and activating these hopes will always be a social act. Ibn 'Arabi has also written that the Mahdi works and is present through his helpers, and each and every one of us should strive to become such a helper of the Saviour. Likewise, Shi'a tradition says that the Mahdi will become present when 313 just and righteous people uphold his mission on Earth. What it means to be truly just and righteous is something that every generation of humankind is negotiating anew. But I personally believe that none of these negotiations will be able to do justice to their purpose if they do not include the utmost multiplicity and plurality of human experience.

It is for this purpose that I share my story and try to make my voice heard. And it is my prayer that it will be joined by a chorus of countless other stories and voices.

NOTES

2. THE UNBEARABLE WHITENESS OF BEING

1. For an interesting analysis of how people of Afghan origin occupy multiple spaces of local belonging and otherness in Delhi, see Sahil K. Warsi, *Being and Belonging in Delhi: Afghan individuals and communities in a global city*. PhD thesis. SOAS University of London (2015).

3. EUNUCHS, SHEMALES, TRANSSEXUALS

1. See previous discussion of the problems of this logic in South Asian contexts—e.g. where *khwajasaras* did not traditionally see themselves as women.
2. Kathryn Ringrose, *The Perfect Servant: Eunuchs and the Social Construction of Gender in Byzantium* (Chicago: University of Chicago Press, 2007), p. 219.
3. Shaun Marmon, *Eunuchs and Sacred Boundaries in Islamic Society* (New York: Oxford University Press, 1995), p. 63.
4. David Ayalon, *Eunuchs, Caliphs and Sultans: A Study of Power Relationships* (Jerusalem: Magnes, 1999), p. 34.
5. Mrs. Meer Hassan Ali, *Observations on the Mussalmauns of India: Descriptive of their Manners, Customs, Habits and Religious Opinions. Made During a Twelve Years' Residence in*

their Immediate Society (1832), second edn. (1917), edited by Frances W. Pritchett, letter 03. Available at: http://www. columbia.edu/itc/mealac/pritchett/00islamlinks/mrsmeerhas-sanali/index.html#index

4. THE GENDERS OF ISLAM

1. Siraj Wahab, 'We Are Neither Men Nor Women, But Muslims Like Anyone Else', *Arab News*, 20 December 2007: https:// www.arabnews.com/node/306907
2. Ibid.
3. Gayatri Reddy, *With Respect to Sex: Negotiating Hijra Identity in South India* (Chicago: Chicago University Press, 2005).
4. British Library manuscript MSS Eur D155, 'Eunuchs or Pawyus of Cutch' by Alex Burnes, Lt. in the Bombay Army and Member Literary Society of Bombay, written in Bombay on 5 September 1829.
5. Everett K. Rowson, 'The Effeminates of Early Medina', *Journal of the American Oriental Society* 11:4 (1991), pp. 671–693.
6. Scott Siraj al-Haqq Kugle, *Homosexuality in Islam. Critical Reflections on Gay, Lesbian and Transgender Muslims* (Oxford: Oneworld, 2010).
7. Skovgaard-Peterson has translated the *fatwa* in *Sex Change in Cairo: Gender and Islamic Law* (1995).
8. 'On the Inner Knowledge of Spirits Made of an Igneous Mixture', Chapter 9 of the *Futūhāt al-Makkiyya*, translated by Gracia López Anguita, *Journal of the Muhyiddin Ibn Arabi Society* 44 (2008): https://ibnarabisociety.org/jinn-spirits-futuhat-al-makkiyya-chapter-9-garcia-lopez-anguita/
9. Translated as *Knowing the Spirit* by James Winston Morris (New York: University of New York Press, 2007), p. 100.
10. Saqer A. Almarri, '"You Have Made Her a Man among Men": Translating the Khuntha's Anatomy in Fatimid Jurisprudence', *Transgender Studies Quarterly* 3:3–4 (2016), p. 581.

11. Khaled El-Rouayheb, *Before Homosexuality in the Arab Islamic World, 1500–1800* (Chicago: University of Chicago Press, 2005), p. 65.
12. Sara Scalenghe, *Disability in the Ottoman World, 1500–1800* (Cambridge: Cambridge University Press, 2014), pp. 147–149.
13. Afsaneh Najmabadi, *Professing Selves: Transsexuality and Same-Sex Desire in Contemporary Iran* (Durham, NC: Duke University Press, 2013).

5. ON THE PATH OF THE SAINTS

1. J.R.I. Cole, *Roots of North Indian Shi'ism in Iran and Iraq* (Berkeley: University of California Press, 1988).
2. See Scott Siraj al-Haqq Kugle, *When Sun Meets Moon: Gender, Eros and Ecstasy in Urdu Poetry* (Chapel Hill: University of North Carolina Press, 2016).
3. Claire Pamment, 'Performing Piety in Pakistan's Transgender Rights Movement', *Transgender Studies Quarterly* 6:3 (2019), p. 310.

7. LET'S TALK ABOUT SEX

1. Zia Jaffrey, *The Invisibles* (New York: Pantheon Books, 1996), pp. 171–2.

8. CRIME AND PREJUDICE

1. Arundhati Roy, 'The NGO-ization of resistance', *Massalijn*, 2014.
2. Glen W. Wright, 'NGOs and Western Hegemony: Causes for Concern and Ideas for Change', *Development in Practice* 22:1 (2012), p. 129.

9. ISLAMISM AND ISLAMOPHOBIA

1. See, for example, 'The Future of the Global Muslim Population' by the Pew Forum on Religion and Public Life (2011), which estimated that falling birth rates would mean that the growth rate of the world's Muslim population would fall from 2.2 per cent a year from 1990–2010 to 1.5 per cent from 2011–2030.

10. SEX AND THE COSMOPOLIS

1. Shahab Ahmed, *What Is Islam?: The Importance of Being Islamic* (Princeton, NJ: Princeton University Press, 2016).
2. David Graeber, 'There Never Was a West: Or, Democracy Emerges from the Spaces in Between', in *Possibilities: Essays on Hierarchy, Rebellion, and Desire*, ed. by David Graeber (Oakland, CA: AK Press, 2007), p. 348.
3. Sa'adi Shirazi, 'Bani Adam', *Gulistān*, chapter 1, story 10. Written circa 1258 CE.
4. Rasul Miller, 'The Black American Sufi: A History', *Sapelo Square*, 18 March 2020: https://sapelosquare.com/2020/03/18/the-black-american-sufi-a-history/